W9-DJM-042

BEDROOM STYLE,
Perfectly Pieced

5 STYLES, 10 PATTERNS, 50 QUILTS

APRIL ROSENTHAL

Published in 2014 by Lucky Spool Media, LLC

www.luckyspool.com
info@luckyspool.com

Text © April Rosenthal

Editor Susanne Woods

Illustrations Courtney Kyle
(pages 114-115 by Alison Glass)

Designer Liz Quan

All rights reserved. No part of this book may be reproduced in any form or by any means, electronic, or mechanical, including photocopying, recording, or by any information storage and retrieval system without permission in writing from the publisher.

The information in this book is accurate and complete to the best of our knowledge. All recommendations are made without guarantee on the part of the author of Lucky Spool Media, LLC. The author and publisher disclaim any liability in connection with this information.

Note to copy shops: Pages 44, 81, and 91 can be photocopied for personal use.

The patterns in this book are copyrighted and must not be made for resale.

Photography Credits:

Page 2 © Josh Badger

Page 3, 102, 104, 107, 122 © April Rosenthal

Page 96, 116, 118, 120 © Lauren Hunt

Page 28, 34, 40, 48, 56, 64, 70, 78, 88, 94, 98, 99, 100, 106, 123, 125, 128 © Lucky Spool Media, LLC

All other photography © Gale Zucker

9 8 7 6 5 4 3 2 1

First Edition
Printed and bound in the United States of America

Library of Congress Cataloging-in-Publication Data available upon request

ISBN 978-1-940655-05-5

LSID0015

DEDICATION

To the three people who make my world go around, and love me in all my crazy:

Jacob, for the more-than-half-my-life you've stood by, happy to be the strong one when I am weak, or the calm one when I am agitated, the folder of laundry when I am swamped, and the soft place when I am exhausted. You know my soul, and you are my wings. This, of course, means more to me than can ever be expressed.

Beckham (Little B), for making me a mama, and making sure that no bad guys get us. You are smart, brave, and, most important, kind. I couldn't be more proud. Thank you for all the hugs and kisses, snuggles, and sweet words. There is nothing better in the whole wide world.

Lily, my little bird and famous artist, for your giggle that brings me immense happiness, and for always knowing just how to be sweet. Thank you for loving projects, and insisting I teach you and let you create, and for being bold and fearless in your art. I want to be like you when I grow up.

Thank you, my loves. I am immeasurably blessed.

PROLOGUE

As a designer, I get e-mails all the time from quilters asking for the names and even SKU numbers of particular fabrics I've used in a quilt. Usually, they saw a picture of my quilt online, or on a pattern cover, or in their local quilt shop's trunk show — and something about the way the fabrics work together is *exactly* what they want for their next project. They always express hope that the fabrics are a part of the same "collection," (a group of fabrics designed to work well together). When I respond on occasion that I simply chose fabrics from my stash and that not all of them are available anymore, they seem deflated. They know they like what they see, and they don't know how to re-create it without using the *exact* fabrics shown.

Even more often, I will see a quilter recoil from a technically brilliant pattern because they don't like the fabrics used in the example. "This pattern is cool," they say, "but I would never make it. I hate the fabrics!" They move on from that pattern, and miss the opportunity to make something truly their own with a pattern that drew their eye.

I've found that it's a unique skill to be able to envision a pattern in fabrics that are different from what is shown, and while some people have that kind of vision, most of us use the "choose and hope" method. You know? The method where you grab some fabric, and make the quilt, and hope it will turn out in a pleasing way? My goal with this book is to show you how to take *any* pattern and make it yours. You don't have to like the fabrics the designer chose. Take a good look at the blocks, at the design — and, if the pattern intrigues you, the guidelines, examples, and instruction given in this book will help you make choices that add your personality to the pattern via fabrics you love — and you will end up with a quilt you love, too. Even better, the more you practice choosing your own fabrics, the more skilled your inner vision will become — until you'll barely notice the fabrics on the cover of a quilt pattern. You will be able to picture it in your ideal palette each time, every time.

CONTENTS

INTRODUCTION

The most basic quilt consists of two layers of fabric, something for warmth in between, and some kind of stitching to keep it all together. These quilts can be found the world over, doing what they do best — keeping people warm and safe from the elements. Though quilts have historically and traditionally been a vital part of any bed, the trend toward fast, easy projects leaves many quilters with a treasure trove of beautiful small projects and lap-size quilts while a box-store basic covers their sleeping space.

It is a joke among most professions that their own family goes without, the cobbler's children having no shoes, as the story goes. It happens in the quilting world, too. We create and stitch, piece and bind, yet sometimes forget to extend our talents to our bedrooms where the people we love most can benefit from our skill and intimacy. There cannot be a more comforting refuge place than under something handcrafted.

Naturally, decorating your rooms with handmade items has benefits beyond the sentimental; it also allows you to have custom, designer linens that reflect your tastes, climate, and sensitivities. In a time when utilitarianism and frugality are becoming increasingly more valued, it makes sense to use your skills to sew practical things for your home. Purchased, these custom, high-end pieces would be astronomical in cost.

Creating your own bedding and accessories allows you to consider your own needs and preferences. This can include but is not limited to: colors, designs, fabric substrates, quilt weight, warmth, breathability, allergens, eco-friendliness, and durability. Of course, what you make may also live on to be an heirloom for your children — though in my house, I intend for my quilts to be used through and through.

As you read through this book, pay attention to the styles that draw your attention and take note of what it is you truly love about a quilt. Is it the fabric? The design? The way the striped binding contrasts? The perfect shade of navy, maybe? Each of the ten patterns included here have an additional spread of color options, showing what the quilt would look like made up in other fabrics, other styles. This is designed to help you make a connection with the style that appeals to you most.

I will walk you through some great ways to identify your style, and some tips and tricks for making any quilt pattern fit that style. It is my goal, in these pages, to open your eyes to the amazing difference that choice makes, and help you see just how easy it can be to choose your styles, fabrics, and linens — and how perfectly *you* your bedroom will feel when you do.

The beauty of a quilt pattern lies in its versatility — in the way it can be made differently by every person who takes it as their own. Through fabric, quilting, batting, and backing choices, and even whether binding is cut straight or on the bias, there are literally thousands of ways to make any quilt pattern unique.

There's nothing better than a hobby that is not only beautiful, but also useful. I hope you will find your next project in this book, and that it makes your home even more *you*.

Let's sew!

xoxo

The Style Quiz

Let's start off with a little test, shall we? Don't worry, you can't fail this pop quiz!

Which of the following **wall treatments** would you most like to use in your home?

- **A** Whitewashed clapboard
- **B** Reclaimed barn wood
- **C** Ornate wallpaper
- **D** Neutral, matte paint
- **E** Pastel paint

If you purchased a new **headboard** or bed, it would be made out of:

- **A** Rattan or sea grass
- **B** Stained wood
- **C** Metal
- **D** Bamboo
- **E** Painted wood

Choose one of the following **color palettes**:

- **A** navy, emerald, aqua, seafoam, pale blue, white
- **B** brick red, navy, aqua, off-white, dark brown, saffron
- **C** lime green, fire orange, peacock blue, gold, pomegranate, violet
- **D** gray, olive, taupe, charcoal, white, black
- **E** watermelon, cantaloupe, aqua, lemon, mint, black

You go to your favorite place to make **home decor** purchases. You come home with:

- **A** a throw pillow with wide stripes
- **B** a wooden ladder
- **C** a brass figurine
- **D** a small potted plant
- **E** a piece of vintage cookware

An **ideal vacation** activity for you would be:

- **A** relaxing on the beach
- **B** visiting a historic community
- **C** eating an ethnic food you have never had before
- **D** finding a secluded spot to observe nature
- **E** searching through antique shops

If you could **live** in any of the following places for a year, which would you choose?

- **A** a village on the ocean
- **B** an organic farm
- **C** a large city
- **D** an isolated cabin
- **E** a restored cottage in a small town

Tally up your answers.

If you answered mostly A, you might really enjoy Coastal style.

If you answered mostly B, chances are you will like a Farmhouse style.

If you answered mostly C, Global Eclectic could be the perfect match for you.

If you answered mostly D, you lean toward a Minimal Zen style.

If you answered mostly E, you have a penchant for all things Vintage Retro.

Of course, my silly little quiz isn't all-inclusive (there are many other styles!), and it's possible that you had one of each answer! As I discuss the different style groups in the next few pages, pay close attention to the elements, colors, and fabrics that you love. Those preferences will give you great insight into your style.

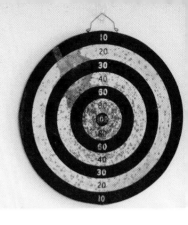

FINDING YOUR STYLE

I am a sucker for personality tests. If a quiz comes up in my Facebook feed, I'm the first to find out which fairy-tale character I most resemble, or what great city I should live in. I have so much fun looking at my results and seeing if I truly could be that character, or live in that city. Even better are the tests that really give me insight. In college I took a Personality Psychology class; besides being fascinating, it gave me the chance to take several professional personality assessments. The results of those tests helped me troubleshoot some areas I could (and still can!) improve, and places where I excel and flourish.

Just like those old personality tests, finding your personal decorating style is a matter of answering some questions, looking at some pictures, thinking through how something makes you feel, and then processing those results into something useful. If it sounds like a lot of work, it is — but in a fun, creative, playful way.

If you share your bedroom with a partner, it is likely that he or she will have opinions and tastes that don't necessarily coincide with yours. I tend to enjoy Global Eclectic, while my husband is staunchly Minimal Zen. These two styles couldn't be more different! Our mutual decor goals aim to be sparse and calm while incorporating pockets of vibrant color as a focal element. This has helped our home truly feel like our own, because it includes both of our tastes and is a reflection of our unique relationship and personalities. Building our space together has been an exercise in compromise — and in the end has been a lot of fun!

If you find yourself in a similar position, consider taking the quiz with your partner to see if you can agree on elements you both enjoy. If that doesn't work, think about what you love most about your chosen style, and ask your partner to do the same. See if you can incorporate each of those into a combined style that suits you both.

STYLE: COASTAL

Water, beaches, the sound of the ocean. Coastal style reflects a lifestyle lived by the water. With lots of blues, greens, and aquas, the color palette is typically limited to the colors naturally found in water and sand — with a lot of heavy white. Decor items often include nautical motifs such as anchors, seashells, ships, and even wild-life like fish, crabs, and lobsters — but to avoid looking kitschy, keep these simple and sparse.

Often, natural fibers like sea grass and palm are used to weave furniture pieces that have a relaxed waterfront feel. This style incorporates texture: think of the differences in the texture of heavy rope, smooth abalone shells, rough coral, rippled water. Coastal style is both relaxed and durable — just like the towns and people who live near the sea. This beautiful variation can be reflected in your quilts by using linen or even textured-looking fabrics in combination with quilting cottons.

One huge component of Coastal style is a heavy infusion of white. Using lots of white in your decor — and in the quilts we will make in Coastal style — mimics the vast light often found in beach homes, and the open sky. Keep your whites really white — veering into creams, eggshells, and off-whites will quickly change the feel of the quilt from Coastal to Colonial.

In your quilt making, be selective about your color palette. Keeping your colors limited to aquas, seafoam greens, and perhaps light taupe or gray will help evoke the light and airy feel of the coast. If you're more interested in a bold nautical feel, consider using navy fabrics only, set on a white background.

As I chose fabrics for the Coastal style quilts in this book, I avoided fabrics with obvious floral motifs or large novelty themes. I used small-scale fabrics and solids so that the overall feel of the quilt is crisp and simple. This style has a relaxed feel, so the fabrics you select shouldn't be fussy, or so bold and busy that they draw visual attention. I've suggested some Coastal color options entirely from solids for this very reason. If you choose patterned fabrics, pick ones that are largely one color, without a lot of contrasting colors or design elements. Use small- to medium-scale prints, geometrics, dots, and, of course, stripes.

In the end, Coastal style is about whatever evokes a relaxed, breezy feeling for you. If there's an octopus print calling your name, by all means, include it in your quilt. Use my guidelines to get started, and rely on what you are drawn to personally to make the final choices.

STYLE: FARMHOUSE

Classic, timeless, and welcoming, Farmhouse style has understated charm. With rich colors and time-worn accessories, this style is both relaxed and infused with sentiment. This style utilizes fabrics, colors, and designs that have lasted through decades, even centuries. The Farmhouse style has its roots in utility. Historically, a farmhouse was the center of a large, working operation — often without many resources to spare. Objects were used until they wore out, even if they were dated or dinged up. Most things were made from sturdy, long-lasting materials that could be used for many years.

Modern Farmhouse style adopts cues from this legacy, where utility, everyday life, and history are central themes. Extraneous objects seem only to clutter this style — it is important to choose one or two great metal, wood, or ceramic pieces, and leave open spaces clear. If a final touch is needed, simple fresh wildflowers are the perfect touch.

Keep the color palette classic: brick red, navy blue, cream, saffron yellow, dusty teal, plum, even avocado. It is common to see colors that are a little more "dusty" in the Farmhouse style, though classic bold colors can also be used (think red, white, and blue patriotic quilts). If you like adding elements of romance or Cottage style, use muted florals and small-scale tonal prints. Look for colors that "have been around the block," as my mom likes to say — meaning, head away from the trendy colors, and stick with classic.

When selecting fabrics, choose tone-on-tone fabrics, herringbone, houndstooth, small stripes, small- and medium-scale florals, damasks, even toiles. If polka dots are used, go with small or even micro dots.

Make it scrappy! In true make-it-do fashion, many Farmhouse style quilts are made with a variety of different fabrics, sometimes so many different prints that they aren't repeated within the quilt. Making a scrappy quilt can be done in any style, but scrap quilts are particularly suited to Farmhouse style — where utility and "Waste Not, Want Not" attitude is held in high esteem. Both background and colored fabrics can be scrappy; many classic quilts use dozens of different fabrics instead of repeating the same fabrics in each block.

To reflect a Farmhouse style, use what you have, and make a quilt that feels timeless and classic. Choose fabrics that evoke a feeling of history and warmth.

STYLE: GLOBAL ECLECTIC

Global Eclectic style can be as diverse as the cultures that span the globe. With so many beautiful sights and experiences, the goal is to mix and match elements from many different cultures to create a cohesive, well-traveled look. This style is packed with information and inspiration informed by a desire to seek out meaningful objects from a variety of cultures. The vibrant colors, eclectic accessories, and rich woven textures make for a visual and emotional experience that is both wildly exhilarating and exotic.

Colors are bold and saturated, and lean toward warmer bright tones of rich, deep browns and purples. Magenta, violet, persimmon, mustard, lime, and eggplant are all good examples of colors in this style. Unlike the reliance on scale and texture in the Coastal and Farmhouse styles, a cohesive Global Eclectic look is achieved by using colors in a similar hue range. This style is a busy and vibrant mix of patterns, colors, and objects.

Picture a sea of tents at a flea market, or a stack of beautiful kimonos, or a farmer's market overflowing with unfamiliar produce. The visual experience that these scenes provide is the inspiration for Global Eclectic quilts. Very little, if any, white space is used — and if there happens to be a "background" fabric, it is rarely white or a solid.

When creating a palette, think of spice markets, a busy Hong Kong street, or Rio's Carnaval celebration. Imagine the colors you would see in those places, or search for mood boards online or via Pinterest, and create a palette with those scenes in mind. Consider using an inspiring picture of one of these events or places, selecting colors directly from the photo to inform your color choices. For a hint of moodiness and mystery, include one darker fabric like a deep navy, eggplant, brown, or black.

Fabric choices for Global Eclectic quilts can be as varied as the experiences they represent. As you are choosing your fabrics, forgo white and light-colored fabrics in favor of rich, saturated, even loud prints. Ornate damasks (in contrasting tones), irreverent multi-color stripes, vibrant shot cottons, eclectic geometrics, and even unusual silks and brocades are perfect choices.

Plan your quilt so there is very little visual resting space, employing a cacophony of competing color voices and prints. The best way to see a culture is to truly be immersed in it. Try to create a quilt that demands the attention of anyone who sees it, and engulfs them in color, texture, and ornamentation.

STYLE: **MINIMAL ZEN**

Grounded, meditative, natural, and calm. The Minimal Zen style is all about creating a space that feels peaceful, harmonious, and organic. Neutral and earth-tone colors with few embellishments are featured. Furniture is usually low to the ground and very functional, without ornamental touches or curved lines. Most decor takes the form of living plants and natural objects such as stones, grasses, and reeds, even sand or gravel. Often, Minimal Zen decor incorporates running water into the environment, as well as large windows if an inspiring natural view is available.

Stark emptiness and order is a hallmark of this style. Large walls without pictures, open horizontal surfaces, streamlined or even hidden appliances. Each object in a minimal environment has a distinct and useful purpose; knickknacks and tchotchkes have no place here. Everyday living necessities are stowed away for a clean, uncluttered look. In quilt making, this translates to large amounts of background or negative space.

The earthy colors of Minimal Zen style reflect nature: cream, beige, brown, olive green, black, gray, charcoal. Using only one or two of these colors, in varying shades, throughout the space is effective. The resulting environment is soothing and cohesive, allowing those who visit to experience a calm and restful place without visual distraction.

For a focal point, use one infusion of a saturated color — often a leaf green, kumquat orange, or bold red. If a focal color is used, it is important to use *only* this color, and only a few times; limit the palette of the rest of the room to one or two layered earth tones. Be mindful of this when selecting fabrics for your quilt to determine if a focal color should be used in the quilt itself or through accessories.

When choosing fabrics, use restraint. Consider using solids, linens, and organic textures. Avoid florals, whites, and bold geometrics. The goal is to use fabrics that have subtle differences in print, color, or texture, so that they blend and flow together and direct the eye across the entire composition. Strive for harmony. If a focal color is used in the quilt itself, consider using a single tonal print (and use it sparingly).

To achieve a modern Minimal and less Zen look, more than one focal color can be used. (See the Intersect quilt on page 70). Applying additional colors to a minimal design adds more modern energy, and removes some of the calmness and Zen feel. If this technique is used, I suggest using solid or near-solid fabrics. Adding prints and patterns can create visual clutter.

VINTAGE RETRO

Sherbet colors, antique Pyrex cook-ware, floral fabrics, and nostalgia are the perfect ingredients for a Vintage

Retro feel. A throwback to the era between the 1930s and 1960s, Vintage Retro style encompasses the iconic and idealistic motifs of those times.

This style embraces sorbet-colored furniture, appliances, and walls. Decor might include found treasures such as antique soda signs, old-fashioned clocks, and painted or enameled buckets and baskets. It lends itself well to thoughtful collections in coordinated colorways or textures, and often includes trinkets from a favorite historical product, brand, or celebrity.

Furniture is often painted white, or any number of candy colors: peach, cotton candy pink, light aqua, lime green, lemon yellow, and cherry red are common choices. For a more "sock hop" feel, designers choose to incorporate a small black or chrome accent, often in flooring. In kitchens, appliances are typically also colored or chrome. Whenever natural elements are used, the colors tend to be blond or honey-colored instead of the darker tones found in Global Eclectic or Minimal Zen styles.

Antique items are used to evoke a feeling of nostalgia, and it is common to see small collections of vintage ephemera all together. Think jars of clothespins, wooden spools in a thrifted retro bowl, buttons in a basket, even vintage glass doorknobs used as coat

hooks. Vintage Retro style finds its charm in the details. "Cute" is definitely at home here.

Floral patterns take center stage in Vintage Retro style, in nearly all shapes and sizes. From small, ditsy daisy prints to bigger blooms on feedsacks, a large portion of prints in this decor style has something to do with flowers. If not flowers, then surely polka dots, or novelty items revolving around the domestic arts — think tiny iron silhouettes, reproduction fabrics that imitate vintage ads, or adorable (and tiny) characters found on Japanese novelty prints. If geometric prints are used, the motif is generally ½" or smaller and remains a simple combination of squares, circles, or basic lines. Gingham is also a common staple in this style.

When choosing fabrics, pastel colors are perfect: pinks, peaches, yellows, and aquas, with a little red for good measure — for a 1950s feel. To achieve a more 1930s feel, lavender and sky blue can be added.

Vintage Retro style is all about nostalgia and remembering happy, simpler times past. Be sure to incorporate fabrics and colors that have you reminiscing and enjoying history.

Coastal

HORIZON

Clean, crisp horizontal lines make a beautiful quilt that whispers of the sea. With minimal piecing, this quilt is perfectly suited for incorporating different substrates and textures. Consider using linen, cotton voile, or even velveteen for contrast and visual interest.

Finished Quilt: 90" x 90"

Pieced and Quilted by April Rosenthal

MATERIALS

White Solid: 5⅓ yards

Aqua 1: ½ yard

Aqua 2: ½ yard

Aqua 3: 1⅛ yard

Aqua 4: ¼ yard

Aqua 5: ½ yard

Aqua 6: 1 yard

Backing Fabric: 8 yards 42"-wide or 2 ¾ yards 108"-wide

Binding Fabric: ¾ yards aqua print

Batting: 96" x 96"

Water Soluble Marker

TIP: Many manufacturers make 108"-wide backing fabric, which doesn't need to be pieced to back even very large quilts and is usually a lighter weight than standard quilting cotton. In addition, it is significantly more cost effective. For each of the quilts in this book, approximately 3 yards of 108"-wide backing can be substituted for the backing yardage listed.

If you choose fabrics that have a distinctive repeat and you want your stripes to look continuous, purchase more of that fabric than called for so that you can fussy cut your strips to match up the repeat when piecing.

CUTTING

From White Solid, cut:
(1) 38½" x 90½" strip
(1) 10½" x 90½" strip
(1) 9½" x 90½" strip
(1) 5½" x 90½" strip

From Aqua 1, cut:
(2) 4½" x 40" strips
(1) 4½" x 11½" strip

From Aqua 2, cut:
(2) 4" x 40" strips
(1) 4" x 11½" strip

From Aqua 3, cut:
(3) 12½" x 40" strips

From Aqua 4, cut:
(2) 2½" x 40" strips
(1) 2½" x 11½" strip

From Aqua 5, cut:
(2) 5" x 40" strips
(1) 5" x 11½" strip

From Aqua 6, cut:
(2) 10½" x 40" strips
(1) 10 ½" x 11½" strip

From Binding Fabric, cut:
(10) 2½" x 42" strips

PIECING

All aqua strips will be sewn together into long strips of the same fabric. Alternate the order you sew pieces together to avoid a more obvious long vertical seam line in your quilt top.

Aqua 1 pieces:
Stitch together lengthwise to make (1) 4½" x 90½" strip. Press seams open.

From Aqua 2 pieces:
Stitch together lengthwise to make (1) 4" x 90½" strip. Press seams open. This strip will be attached to the quilt top using raw-edge appliqué. If desired, trim top and bottom edges with pinking shears or pinking rotary cutter for even fraying.

From Aqua 4 pieces:
Stitch together lengthwise to make (1) 2½" x 90½" strip. Press seams open.

From Aqua 5 pieces:
Stitch together lengthwise to make (1) 5" x 90 ½" strip. Press seams open. This strip will be attached to the quilt top using raw-edge appliqué. See Aqua 2 (above).

From Aqua 6 pieces:
Stitch together lengthwise to make (1) 10½" x 90½" strip. Press seams open.

From Aqua 3 pieces:

1 Stitch together lengthwise to make (1) 12½" x approximately 119" strip. Press seams open.

2 Fold strip in half and mark the center with a pin at the top and bottom of the strip. Using a water-soluble fabric marker and a ruler, mark the center line.

3 Mark additional vertical lines spaced 2½" from either side of the center line, continuing to each raw edge.

4 Measure and mark the horizontal center line, then make additional horizontal lines spaced 2½" from either side of the center line, continuing to each raw edge. **(Fig. 1)**

Figure 1

5 Fold strip on vertical center line, wrong sides together. Press. With matching thread, stitch ¼" away from the fold.

6 Open strip. Fold the strip on the vertical line to the right of your center pleat. Press. Stitch ¼" away from the fold. **(Fig. 2)**

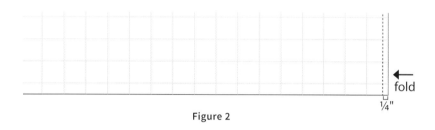

fold

¼"

Figure 2

7 Continue folding, pressing, and stitching each marked vertical line until all pleats have been stitched into place. **(Fig. 3)**

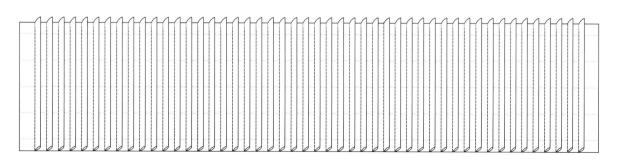

Figure 3

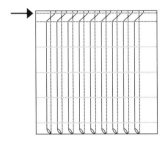

Figure 4

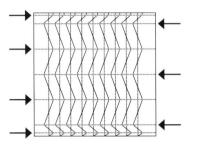

Figure 5

8 Staystitch horizontally from left to right ⅛" from the top of the strip. All the pleats should be stitched down with the folds on the right. (Fig. 4)

9 Stitch from right to left on the first marked horizontal line, stitching folded flaps to the left. Flaps will now be stitched in the opposite direction to Step 8. (Fig. 5)

10 Continue stitching rows in alternating directions until all marked horizontal lines have been stitched. Change directions one more time and staystitch ⅛" from the bottom of the strip.

11 Trim strip to 90½" long.

TIP: When stitching a long seam, I suggest using a walking foot attachment on your machine. In fact, I almost never change to another presser foot! A walking foot attachment will pull the fabric evenly from the top and the bottom, preventing the fabric from stretching and shifting.

PUTTING IT TOGETHER

1 Match ends and centers of Aqua 1 strip and white 10½" strip. Pin along raw edge every 3". Stitch strips together. Press toward Aqua 1 strip.

2 On the right side of the fabric, with a water soluble marker, draw a horizontal line ⅜" **above** the seam of the Aqua 1 strip. Using a fabric glue stick or pins, align the top raw edge of the Aqua 2 strip with the drawn line. Stitch ¼" from top edge leaving top edge raw.

3 Stitch ¼" from bottom raw edge of Aqua 2 strip. (Fig. 6)

4 Sew Aqua 3 and 4 strips together lengthwise. Press toward darker fabric. (Fig. 7)

5 Sew 9½" white strip to Aqua 6 strip. Press toward the darker fabric.

6 Repeat Steps 2 and 3 for the Aqua 5 and 6 strips, this time marking a line ⅜" **below** the seam on the Aqua 6 fabric.

7 Sew all sections together, including the top (38½" wide) and bottom (5½" wide) white strips, as shown in Figure 8.

FINISHING

Layer, baste, quilt, and bind using your preferred methods.

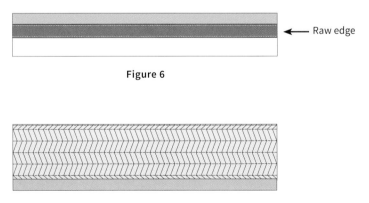

Figure 6

← Raw edge

Figure 7

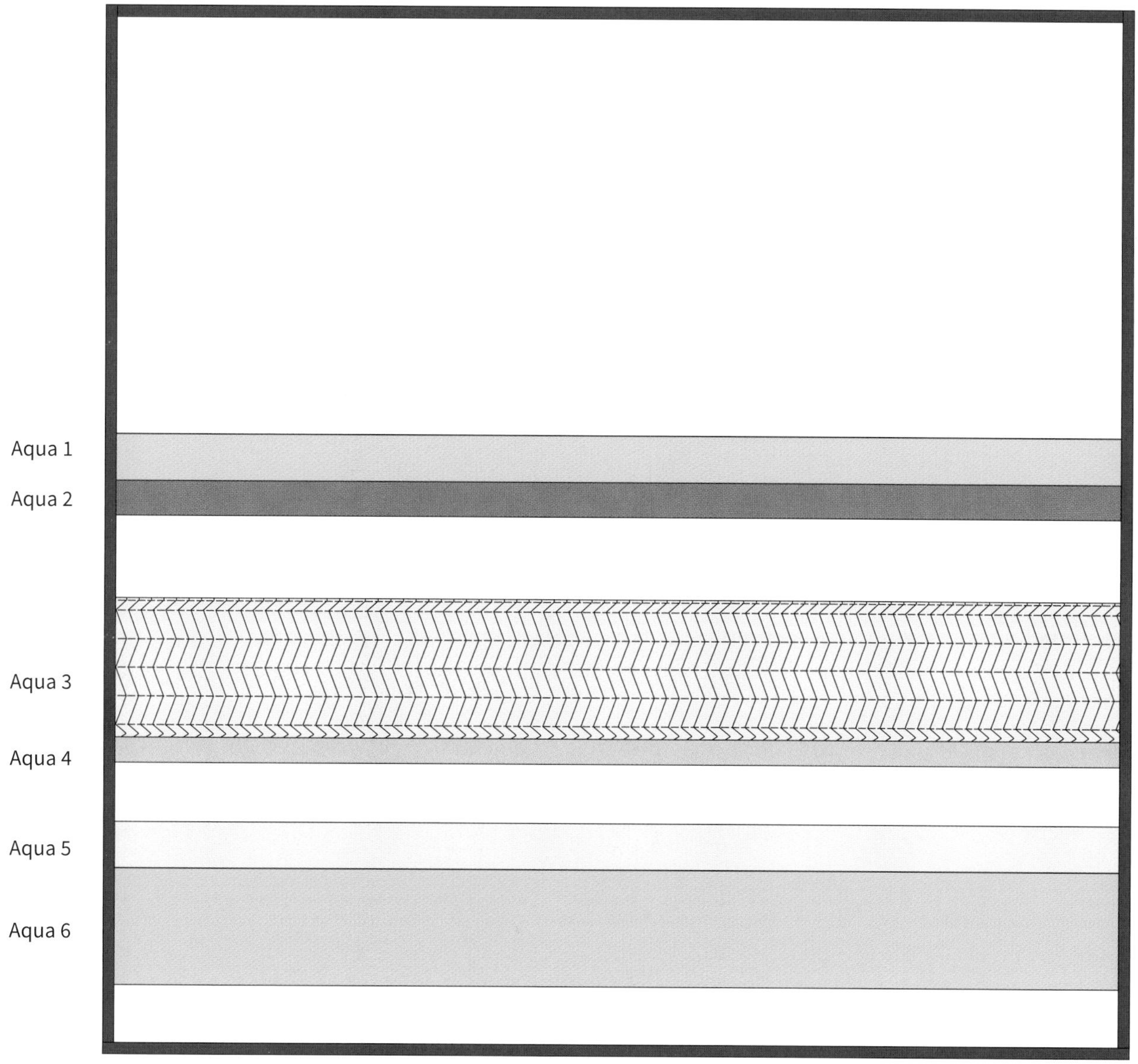

Aqua 1
Aqua 2
Aqua 3
Aqua 4
Aqua 5
Aqua 6

Figure 8

GLOBAL ECLECTIC

Bright, saturated prints can be used for an eclectic feel, too. With an ornate background print and coordinating tonal prints used as the strips, this Global look is festive and summery, like a beautiful Caribbean town. Remember, Global Eclectic-style is all about what is evocative for you — what makes you remember places you've been or places you dream of seeing.

FARMHOUSE

This beautiful version features some of my favorite navy and red prints for a great traditional and oh-so-classic interpretation. This quilt reminds me of fireworks, parades, and the hometown charm of Independence Day — and isn't that what this style of quilts to do? Remind us of the past, and things that are important to us? I'd say spending time with family and celebrating our heritage are two things that fall into those categories.

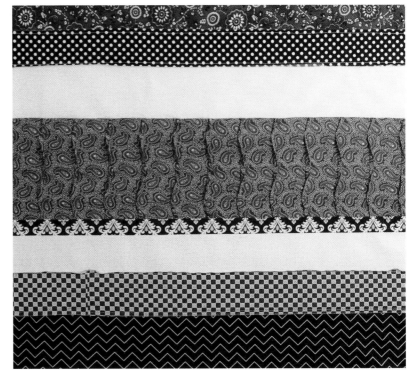

MINIMAL ZEN

This might be one of my favorite Minimal Zen color options in this entire book. The earthy gray and eggplant tones with a sprout green for contrast create an organic and meditative look and feel. Accessorized with a few pretty solid or even metallic-accented pillows, a bed made with this quilt is just stunning.

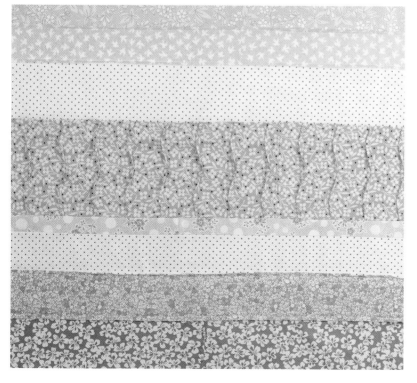

VINTAGE RETRO

A fast and easy way to get just the right vintage prints for your quilt is to head to your favorite quilt shop and ask them to point you in the direction of their 1930s reproduction fabrics. These fabrics have been re-created from scans of original fabrics dating from the 1930s and are sure to make your quilt authentically retro!

BREAKING TIDE

I pieced this quilt by putting all the pieces into a large basket and pulling them out randomly. I wanted to let the fabrics and colors intermingle without too much planning. The result is organic and free, like breaking waves on the shoreline.

Finished Quilt: 92½" x 92½"

Pieced by Julie Broadbent;
Quilted by April Rosenthal

MATERIALS

White Solid: 3¼ yards

Seven Blue, Aqua, Green, or Seafoam fabrics: 1 yard each

Backing Fabirc: 8½ yards 42"-wide, or 2¾ yards 108"-wide

Binding Fabric: ¾ yards

Batting: 99" x 99"

Fine-tip pen

TIP: When stitching quarter-square triangles together, you may have to re-press a seam here and there to ensure that your pieces nest well. The extra time and effort is worth it to have nice, flat, well-matched seams.

CUTTING

From White Solid, cut:
(15) 13½" squares

(10) 4½" x 40" strips for border

From Blue, Green, Aqua, and Seafoam fabrics, cut:
(5) 13½" squares from each fabric, for a total of 35 squares

From Binding Fabric, cut:
(10) 2½" x 42" strips

PIECING

1 Mark a diagonal line from corner to corner on a random selection of 25 of the squares. **(Fig. 1)**

2 Randomly pair one marked square with one unmarked square. Place right sides together and stitch ¼" away from both sides of the drawn line. **(Fig. 2)**

3 Repeat until you have a total of 25 paired units.

4 Cut along the drawn line. **(Fig. 3)** Press lightly toward darker fabric.

5 Cut each pieced square in half diagonally, perpendicular to your seam line. **(Fig. 5)** Randomly pair 2 units, placing right sides together and nesting seams. **(Fig. 6)** Stitch on long side. Press seam to the side. Trim to 12½".

PUTTING IT TOGETHER

1 Stitch blocks together in 7 rows of 7 blocks. You will have one leftover block. Press seams to the side, alternating direction by row. Stitch rows together, nesting seams. Press seams to the side.

2 Piece 4½" white border strips together as needed. Attach along the sides first and trim, then press toward border. Repeat for the top/bottom borders. **(Fig. 7)**

FINISHING

Layer, baste, quilt, and bind your quilt using your preferred methods.

Figure 1

Figure 2

Figure 3

Figure 4

Figure 5

Figure 6

Figure 7

make it your style

FARMHOUSE

Is there anything more classic than brick red, golden yellow, and navy blue? These "primary" colors in small-scale prints are a traditional and comfortable color palette that is perfectly at home in a farmhouse. I chose a tonal cream and white floral for the border to add a little texture and cottage style.

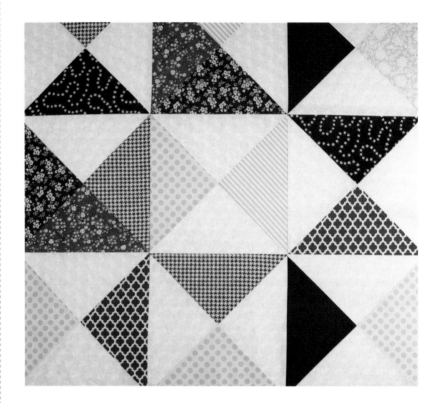

MINIMAL ZEN

For this beautiful and very calming version, I chose several gray and white fabrics with mid-scale prints in organic patterns. Though there are quite a few prints, the overall feel remains minimal because of the severely limited color palette and the similarity in scale of designs. No one fabric stands out. I completed this version with a gray solid for the borders.

GLOBAL ECLECTIC

Deep, saturated linens and vibrant prints make for a textured and lively quilt that is intriguing and exotic. The solid linens add depth, texture, and a visual respite from the colorful prints while still maintaining a global feel that could not be replicated with a single solid color.

VINTAGE RETRO

Bright feedsack prints in sunny colors set against a cream neutral make for a fun and very retro interpretation of Breaking Tide. When choosing reproduction prints be careful to keep your color choices light and bright — or, if you choose to lean more toward dark reproduction prints, your finished quilt will have a more Civil War era feel.

Farmhouse

SUMMER FIELDS

This quilt is perfect for using your scraps. It is organized simply by laying out squares on a design wall or floor and stitching those squares together in offset rows. There are no blocks to make. Organization is the name of the game for this quilt so be sure to keep a record of your color layout before you begin piecing.

Finished Quilt: 90" x 90"

Pieced and Quilted by April Rosenthal

MATERIALS

From Fabirc Scraps: 4½" squares totalling 4 yards

Background Fabric: 1⅔ yards

Border Fabirc: 2 yards

Binding Fabric: ¾ yard

Backing Fabric: 8 yards

Batting: 96" x 96"

CUTTING

From Fabric Scraps, cut:
(244) 4½" squares
(12) 2½" x 4½" rectangles

From Background Fabric, cut:
(13) 4½" x 42" strips
Subcut:
(107) 4½" squares
(8) 2½" x 4½" rectangles

From Border Fabric, cut:
(9) 7½" x 42" strips

From Binding Fabric, cut:
(10) 2½" x 42" strips

TIP: If you don't have enough scraps to make all the squares, you can use a 5" charm pack or 10" layer cake to quickly add lots of prints to your project.

PIECING

1 Using Figures 1 and 2 as a reference, lay out your scrappy and background squares so that colors and fabrics are distributed in a way that you love.

2 Use your cell phone, tablet, or a digital camera to take a quick snap-shot of your entire quilt layout. You can refer back to it anytime to make sure things are all in order.

3 Gather the pieces for each row. Start with the top left corner with a 2½" x 4½" rectangle and work your way across the first row from left to right, placing each subsequent piece of the row at the bottom of your stack and ending with a 2½" x 4½" rectangle. For the second row, begin and end with a 4½" square. Repeat for each row alternating beginning and ending with a 2½" x 4½" rectangle or a 4½" square. Number the rows and pin to the top of each row's pile.

4 Piece together the squares in each row, pressing seams toward the darker color.

5 Sew the rows together, pinning as needed. Remember that the squares in each row are offset from the rows above and below, like brickwork. Press.

6 Piece 7½" border strips together as needed. Attach the right and left sides first as shown in Figure 2 and trim as necessary. Press toward border.

7 Repeat with the top and bottom border strips.

FINISHING

Layer, baste, quilt, and bind using your preferred methods.

Figure 1

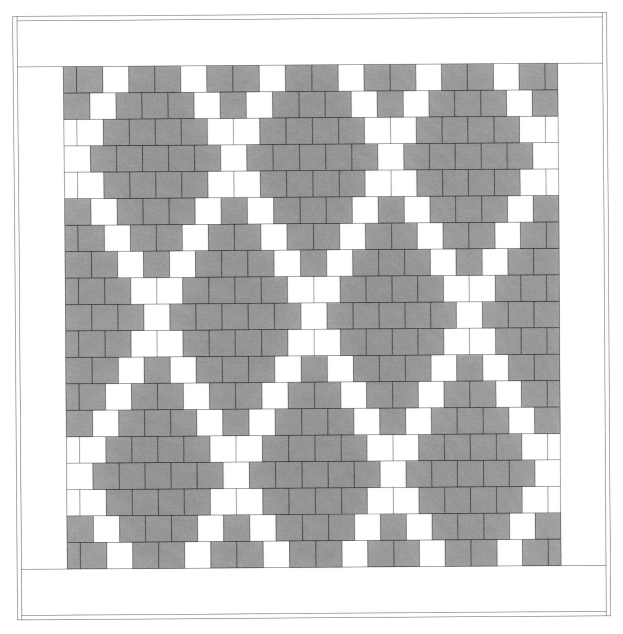

Figure 2

make it your style

COASTAL

Varying shades of blue remind me of a calm beach in late summer. For a drastically different but dashing Coastal look, you may even consider inverting the colors, so that you have various whites as your "scrappy" portion, and a crisp navy background fabric to create the chain.

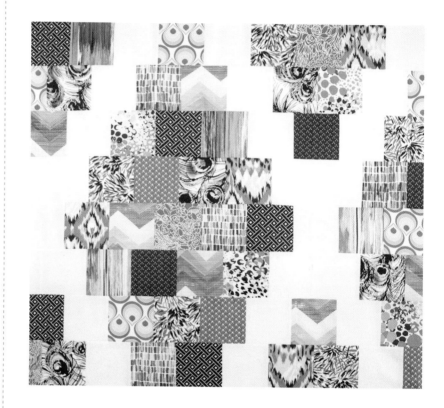

GLOBAL ECLECTIC

The key to making Summer Fields look global and eclectic is the diversity of color you include. For a brilliant quilt that evokes memories of outdoor markets and exotic sights and smells, try a palette of warm orange, red, and gold scraps, with an unexpected chartreuse or magenta thrown in to add a little mystery. Keep your background fabric a dusty cream or taupe, to complete the look.

MINIMAL ZEN

Keeping it simple is the name of the game to get a minimal look using this pattern. Be careful when choosing your fabrics, and include a very limited palette without any sharp contrasts. This will help your quilt retain a Zen feel without losing the interest that comes with the variety of scraps.

VINTAGE RETRO

If a retro look is your style, have fun using your favorite scraps from eras past. Be sure to mix up the scale of your prints, and consider including some coordinating basics (tiny polka dots, simple stripes, or gingham) so that your vintage prints really shine. Keeping large- and mid-scale prints distributed well among more basic fabrics will help to retain distinction between squares and ensure your piecing is noticed.

STARLIGHT SQUARE DANCE

Just like a beautiful meal or a well-planned performance, the key to this quilt is contrast. As you select your fat quarters and lay out your blocks, choose fabrics that differ from each other in scale, color, and design density. This not only helps make a stunning quilt, but also accentuates your hard work and piecing skill by letting each part of the block shine.

Finished Quilt: 89" x 89"

Pieced and Quilted by April Rosenthal

MATERIALS

Fat Quarters (18" x 22"): 25

Sahsing: 1 ½ yards

Sashing Stars: ¾ yard

Post Block Centers: ¼ yard

Inner Border: ⅝ yards

Outer Border: 1½ yards

Backing Fabric: 8 yards 42"-wide, or 2¾ yards 108"-wide

Binding Fabric: ¾ yards

Batting: 95" x 95"

CUTTING

From each Fat Quarter, cut:
(1) 3⅞" square (Piece A)
(4) 3" squares (Piece B)
(4) 3" x 3⅞" rectangles (Piece C)
(2) 4¾" squares, then subcut each square twice on diagonals to make a total of 8 triangles (Piece D)
(4) E pieces using Template E (see page 44)

From Sashing, cut:
(4) 12½" x 42" strips

Subcut:
(40) 4" x 12½" rectangles

From Sashing Stars, cut:
(9) 2¼" x 42" strips

Subcut:
(160) 2¼" squares (18 per strip)
(2) 2⅝" x 42" strips

Subcut:
(32) 2⅝" squares, then subcut each square once on the diagonal to make 64 triangles

From Post Block Centers, cut:
(2) 3" x 42" strips

Subcut:
(16) 3" squares

From Inner Border, cut:
(8) 2½" x 42" strips

From Outer Border, cut:
(9) 6" x 42" strips

From Binding Fabric, cut:
(10) 2½" x 42" strips

CUTTING TIPS

Label each stack of strips and pieces with their place in the quilt by pinning a small sticky note or scrap of fabric to the top piece. This will help you avoid mistakes and be sure of placement as you make your way through the piecing.

If you're unsure about choosing fabrics that will work well together, consider using a pre-cut bundle of 25 fat quarters. The fabrics in these collections are created to coordinate as well as provide enough variety in scale and color to be used in the same project.

PIECING

In this quilt, three different blocks make up the piecing — the Main Blocks, the Pieced Sashing, and the Post Blocks. The Pieced Sashing and Post Blocks make up the secondary pattern of stars at the intersections of the Main Blocks.

MAIN BLOCKS

Each block uses the following pieces:
(1) Piece A: 3⅞" square
(4) Piece B: 3" squares
(4) Piece C: 3" x ⅞" rectangles
(8) Piece D: triangles
(4) Piece E: Template E

1 Mix and match your fabrics so that pieces A, C, and D are each different, but pieces B and E are the same fabric.

2 Referring to Figure 1, first make a center nine-patch with pieces A, B, and C, sewing rows together. Nest the seams and follow the arrows for pressing directions.

3 Referring to Figure 2, piece corner units by sewing a (D) triangle to each side of an (E) piece. Press toward (E). Attach corner units to the nine-patch center and press.

4 Repeat to make a total of 25 main blocks.

PIECED SASHING

1 Mark a diagonal line on the wrong side of (160) 2¼" sashing star squares. Place one square on a corner of a 12½" x 4½" sashing rectangle, right sides together. Stitch on the drawn line. Trim excess to a ¼" and press toward triangle. (**Fig. 3**)

2 Repeat on each corner and on each sashing rectangle for a total of 40 sashing units.

POST BLOCKS

1 Mark the center on all sides of a post block center square (**Fig. 4**) and on the long side on each sashing star triangle. (**Fig. 5**)

2 Aligning center marks, stitch one triangle to one side of a square. Press toward triangle. Repeat for the opposite side of the square overlapping the center tips. (**Fig. 6**)

3 Repeat on remaining sides of the square. (**Fig. 7**)

4 Trim off dog ears if desired.

5 Continue until all squares have been completed, for a total of 16 post blocks.

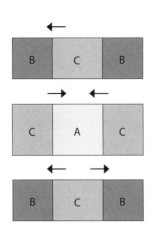

Figure 1

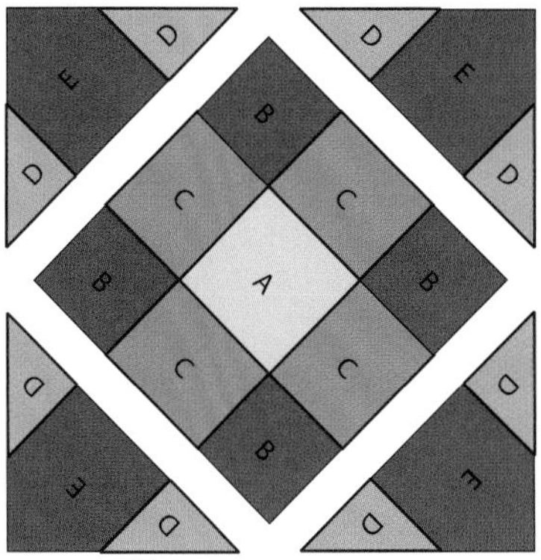

Figure 2

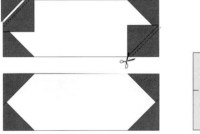

Figure 3

Figure 4

Figure 5

Figure 6

Figure 7

Figure 8

QUILT TOP CONSTRUCTION

1 Lay out quilt on a flat surface or design wall. For Rows 1, 3, 5, 7 and 9 arrange main blocks in 5 rows of 5 blocks each with a pieced sashing rectangle vertically between blocks. For Rows 2, 4, 6 and 8, arrange pieced sashing rectangles horizontally, placing post blocks at pieced sashing intersections. **(Fig. 9)**

2 Take a picture of your layout to use for reference.

3 Beginning with the top left corner, gather your pieces across the row from left to right, putting the next piece at the bottom of the stack. Number each row and pin the number to the top of each row's pile.

4 Piece together the rows, nesting seams and pinning as needed to keep the pieces aligned at intersections and the rows matched up at the ends. Press seams toward sashing.

5 For the first border, piece 2½" inner strips together as needed. Attach along sides first and trim, then press toward border. Repeat for the top/bottom borders. For the next border, piece 6" outer strips together as needed. Attach and trim, then press toward border. **(Fig. 9)**

FINISHING

Layer, baste, quilt, and bind using your preferred methods.

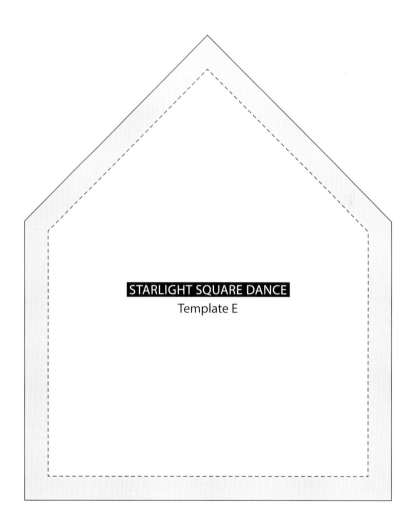

STARLIGHT SQUARE DANCE
Template E

Photocopy at 100%

—— cut line

--- stitch line

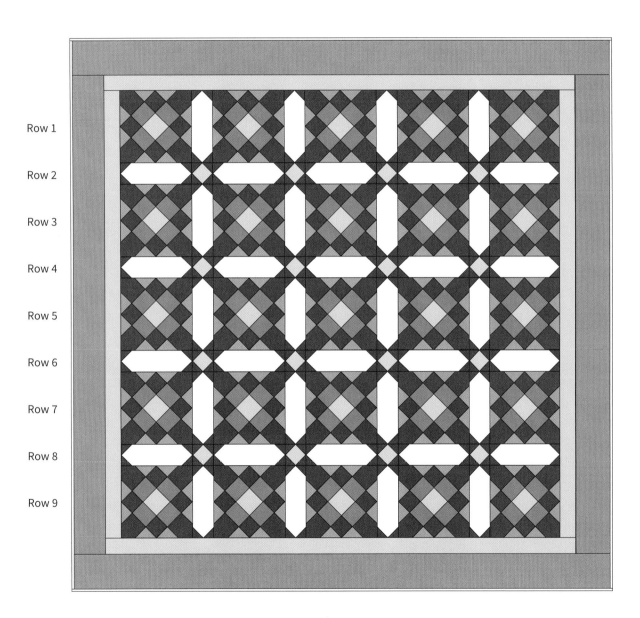

Row 1

Row 2

Row 3

Row 4

Row 5

Row 6

Row 7

Row 8

Row 9

Figure 9

GLOBAL ECLECTIC

When you want your finished quilt to look eclectic, one of the best ways to make that happen is through contrasting patterns. Combining busy prints with saturated color always results in a show-stopping visual experience. Limiting your prints to certain color families will help maintain a sense of cohesion while making sure your piecing doesn't get lost.

COASTAL

Deep nautical aqua and bottle green colors combine with a perfect plaid to make a preppy coastal interpretation. When choosing fabrics for this look, limit your choices to a single busy print (i.e., plaid) and complement that print with other basics. Following this guideline will help your quilt retain a simple, laid-back, waterfront feel.

MINIMAL ZEN

If you want a more minimal and modern look, try using mainly solids to piece your quilt and then incorporating just one print as a focal point. Choose fabrics that will be viewed as a solid but still have beautiful depth and texture, such as wovens, linens, and shot cottons.

VINTAGE RETRO

To get a retro feel in your piecing, you don't have to use "vintage" prints — your color palette can do all the work for you! Try using prints that have classic, timeless motifs like dots or small florals, and choose colors that have a nostalgic feel for you. In this example, I combined robin's egg blue, sunshine yellow, cotton candy pink, and kelly green for a color palette that reminds me of the sorbet-colored prom dresses of the 1950s.

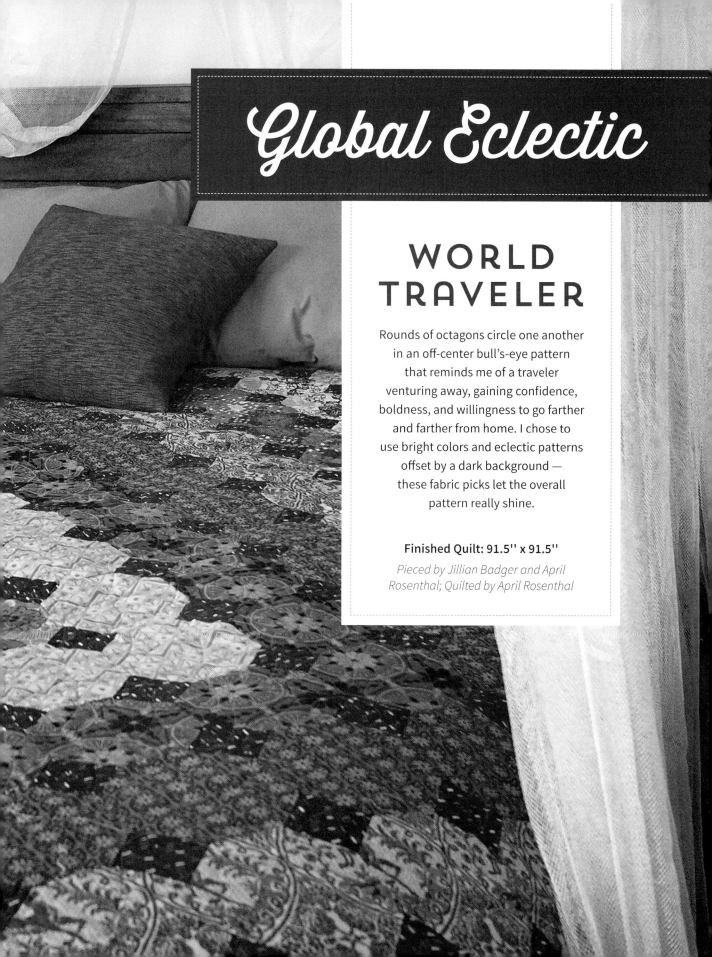

Global Eclectic

WORLD TRAVELER

Rounds of octagons circle one another in an off-center bull's-eye pattern that reminds me of a traveler venturing away, gaining confidence, boldness, and willingness to go farther and farther from home. I chose to use bright colors and eclectic patterns offset by a dark background — these fabric picks let the overall pattern really shine.

Finished Quilt: 91.5'' x 91.5''

Pieced by Jillian Badger and April Rosenthal; Quilted by April Rosenthal

MATERIALS

Reference Figure 4 (see page 52) to label your fabric choices for each round. This will help with cutting the appropriate number of pieces as well as allow you to piece the quilt without laying out the entire thing on the floor or design wall.

Background: 3½ yards

Center Blocks: ¼ yard

Rounds:

⅓ yard for Round 1

½ yard for Round 2

⅔ yard for Round 3

⅔ yard for Round 4

⅔ yard for Round 5

⅔ yard for Round 6

⅔ yard for Round 7

⅔ yard for Round 8

⅔ yard for Round 9

⅔ yard for Round 10

½ yard for Round 11

½ yard for Round 12

⅓ yard for Round 13

⅓ yard for Round 14

Backing Fabric: 8¼ yards 42"-wide or 2¾ yards 108"-wide

Binding Fabric: ¾ yard

Batting: 98" x 98"

CUTTING

From Background Fabric, cut:

(1,244) 2" squares

From Center Blocks, cut:

(4) 5½" squares

From Rounds, cut:

Round 1: cut (12) 5½"' squares

Round 2: cut (20) 5½" squares

Round 3: cut (25) 5½" squares

Round 4: cut (31) 5½" squares

Round 5: cut (32) 5½" squares

Round 6: cut (32) 5½" squares

Round 7: cut (32) 5½"' squares

Round 8: cut (30) 5½" squares

Round 9: cut (27) 5½"' squares

Round 10: cut (21) 5½"' squares

Round 11: cut (16) 5½" squares

Round 12: cut (12) 5½" squares

Round 13: cut (8) 5½" squares

Round 14: cut (9) 5½" squares

From Binding Fabric, cut:

(10) 2½" x 42" strips

TIP: To save time, consider using a die cutter to cut your 5½" and 2" squares. I used mine to cut out the pieces for this quilt in less than an hour. Many companies make fabric die cutters, and some quilt shops even have them to rent. If you're an avid quilter, purchasing a cutting system may be worth the investment; however, you will always need to buy more yardage than the fabric requirements listed as they do produce more waste.

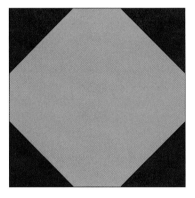

Figure 1

PIECING

With 311 of the same simple block to make, chain piecing is the name of the game.

Traditional Method:

This block is made by marking a diagonal across the back of each 2" square, and then placing one marked square on each corner of a larger square and sewing on the drawn line (**Fig. 1**). To save time, I suggest an alternate Speed Method (see facing page). Select the method that best suits you.

Speed Method:

1 Mark a straight line lengthwise on a 5" piece of blue painter's tape, washi tape, or masking tape. Place the tape on your sewing machine bed with the line directly extending out from the needle. (**Fig. 2**)

2 Place a small (2") square on the corner of a large (5½") square. Start with the corner of the small square under the needle, and the opposite corner aligned with the line on the tape. (**Fig. 3**)

3 Sew, keeping the corner of the small block following the marked line on the tape. Continue sewing until the entire piece passes under the needle.

4 Align your next set of squares under the needle and continue as before.

5 Chain piece all 5½" blocks, with one small square on each corner. Trim excess fabric (**Fig. 1**) and press gently toward the large square.

PUTTING IT TOGETHER

1 Referring to Figure 4 and beginning in the upper left corner of the quilt, make stacks of blocks for each row, labeling them with their row number (1-25). Each row will consist of from 1 to 25 blocks, with the most blocks in Row 13. For example, your first stack (Row 1) should have a single "Round 10" block. Your second stack (Row 2) should have three "Round 9" blocks. Continue making stacks and labeling them until you have all 25 rows ready to sew.

2 Sew together the rows of the quilt from your stacks ensuring your small triangles meet up and referring to Figure 3 as needed. Press seams to the side in alternating directions by row.

3 Piece rows together according to Figure 4, nesting seams. Press.

SQUARING UP

Cut through the top and bottom rows beginning at the top left of the quilt. You will cut through the middle of the top left square and across each pieced square along the horizontal (**Fig. 5**). Repeat for the sides going along the vertical.

FINISHING

Layer, baste, quilt, and bind using your preferred methods.

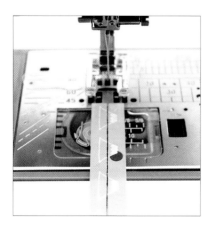

Figure 2

Figure 3

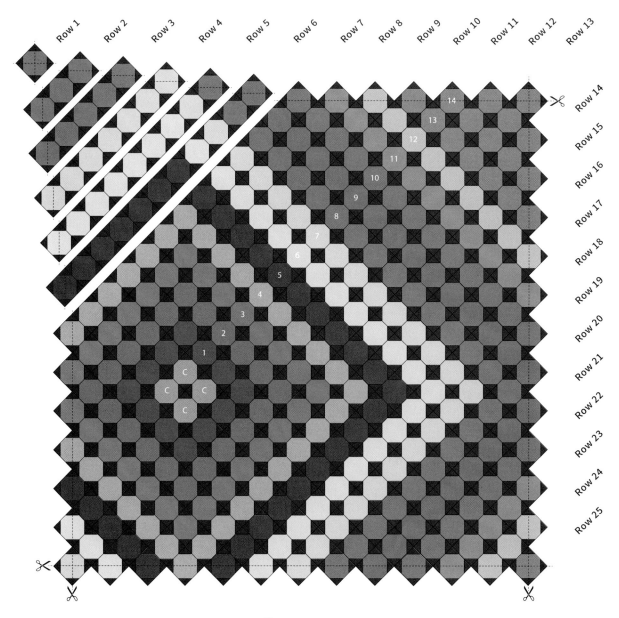

Row 1 Row 2 Row 3 Row 4 Row 5 Row 6 Row 7 Row 8 Row 9 Row 10 Row 11 Row 12 Row 13

Row 14 Row 15 Row 16 Row 17 Row 18 Row 19 Row 20 Row 21 Row 22 Row 23 Row 24 Row 25

Figure 4

Figure 5

COASTAL

For a look that is timeless, classic, and oh-so coastal, try using simple solids in navy and sky blue in alternating rows. Combined with crisp white linens and a bright, airy room, this quilt would be a perfect nautical touch.

FARMHOUSE

Farmhouse quilts can be made more romantic by using muted colors and prominent florals. In this beautiful version of World Traveler, reproductions of French linens in reds and taupes make a quilt that will add a little romance to any farmhouse.

MINIMAL ZEN

For the ultimate in Minimal Zen style, use only black and white prints. Sleek, elegant, and sophisticated, this limited color palette makes it easy to add a few prints without losing the minimal look.

VINTAGE RETRO

Any era can be the inspiration for your Vintage Retro style quilt, as is shown here by this 1960s-inspired version of World Traveler. With bright pink, mushroom, black, lime, and aqua, this is one retro quilt that will catch your eye — and help bring a nostalgic experience to any room.

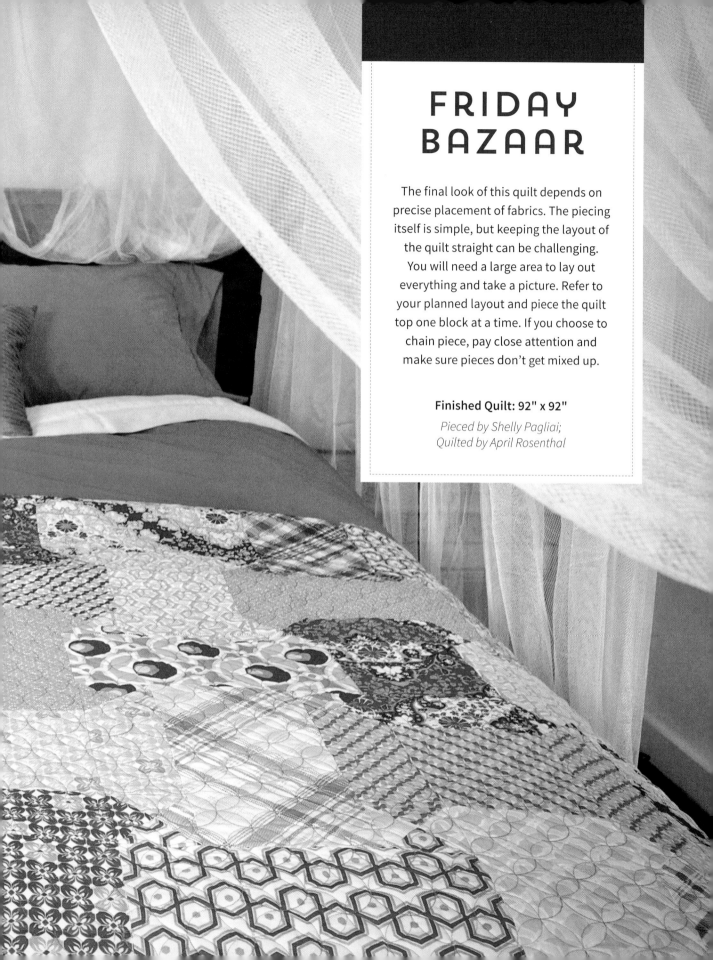

FRIDAY BAZAAR

The final look of this quilt depends on precise placement of fabrics. The piecing itself is simple, but keeping the layout of the quilt straight can be challenging. You will need a large area to lay out everything and take a picture. Refer to your planned layout and piece the quilt top one block at a time. If you choose to chain piece, pay close attention and make sure pieces don't get mixed up.

Finished Quilt: 92" x 92"

Pieced by Shelly Pagliai;
Quilted by April Rosenthal

MATERIALS

Fat Quarters (18" x 22"): 30

    Group A: 15 fat quarters

    Group B: 12 fat quarters

    Group C: 3 fat quarters

Border Fabric: 1¼ yards

Backing Fabric: 8 ¼ yards 42"-wide, or 2¾ yards 108"-wide

Binding Fabric: ¾ yards

Batting: 98" x 98"

CUTTING

From each of 15 Group A Fat Quarters, cut:

(3) 6 ½" x 12½" rectangles

(3) 4¼" squares, then subcut twice on the diagonal to make 16 triangles

From each of 12 Group B Fat Quarters, cut:

(3) 6 ½" squares

(6) 3½" x 6½" rectangles

(3) 4¼'' squares, then subcut twice on the diagonal to make 16 triangles

From each of 3 Group C Fat Quarters, cut:

(6) 3½" x 6½' rectangles

(6) 4¼" squares, then subcut twice on the diagonal to make 24 triangles

(1) 4¼" square from a Group C fabric of your choice, then subcut twice on the diagonal to make 4 triangles

From Border Fabric, cut:

(10) 4½" x 40" strips

From Binding Fabric, cut:

(10) 2½" x 40" strips

PREPARATION

You might want to cut the fat quarters differently depending on which Group they are in. For context, here are some things to consider about each of the Groups:

Group A, 15 Fat Quarters:

This Group will use the largest pieces (rectangles), so large-scale prints and directional fabrics can be used, such as main focus prints, stripes, and any fabric where it is important to keep the motif "right side up." Any prints will work well in this Group.

Group B, 12 Fat Quarters:

This Group uses squares instead of rectangles so will have a mix of small and larger pieces. Most fabrics will work well here.

Group C, 3 Fat Quarters:

This Group will be partial blocks. The pieces will not be as large as the other groups; this is not the place to put your favorite prints.

LAYOUT

Referring to Figure 8, begin by laying out Group A and Group B pieces maintaining the spool shape for each and being careful to distribute the fabrics from the same Fat Quarter. Finish your layout by using Group C rectangles and triangles to fill in the outer edges (**Fig. 1**). Don't forget to take a photo of your layout before sewing the pieces together.

PIECING UNITS

1 Assemble each quarter-square triangle (QST) by stitching adjacent triangles to one another and pressing seams to one side. Sew triangle units together, nesting seams, to make a QST. Press. Square up block to 3½" square. (**Fig. 2**)

2 Continue sewing QSTs together, replacing each in the layout as it is completed to make sure pieces are in the right place. Refer to your photo as needed. (**Fig. 3**)

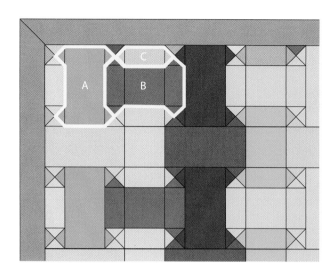

Figure 1

Figure 2

TIP: When you're squaring up quarter-square blocks, make sure you trim so that the center of the block stays in the center. Your points will have a hard time matching up if the blocks aren't cut evenly. Use an acrylic ruler made specifically for squaring up quarter-square triangles, or a square ruler in the size you're trimming to with the center marked.

Figure 3

PUTTING IT TOGETHER

1 Stitch each QST block to the 6 ½" x 3½" rectangle directly above or below it. Press seams toward rectangle. (**Fig. 4**)

2 Stitch each 3½" x 6½" rectangle to the 6½" square directly above or below it in every other column. Press seams toward rectangle. (**Fig. 5**)

3 Sew rows 1, 3, 5, 7, and 9, nesting seams. Press seams away from QST units. (**Fig. 6**)

4 Sew rows 2, 4, 6, and 8, pressing seams toward the 12½" x 6 ½" rectangles. (**Fig. 7**)

5 Sew all rows together, nesting seams. Press toward even numbered rows. (**Fig. 8**)

6 Piece 4½" border strips and attach to quilt, mitering corners if appropriate for your border fabric choice. (**Fig. 8**)

TIP: Mitered borders are a great choice when you have an obvious pattern in your border fabric. Mitering the borders allows the pattern to continue around the quilt instead of being broken up at the intersections of horizontal borders.

FINISHING

Layer, baste, quilt, and bind using your preferred methods.

Figure 4

Figure 5

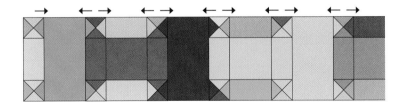

Figure 6

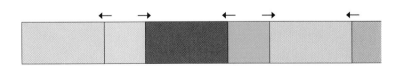

Figure 7

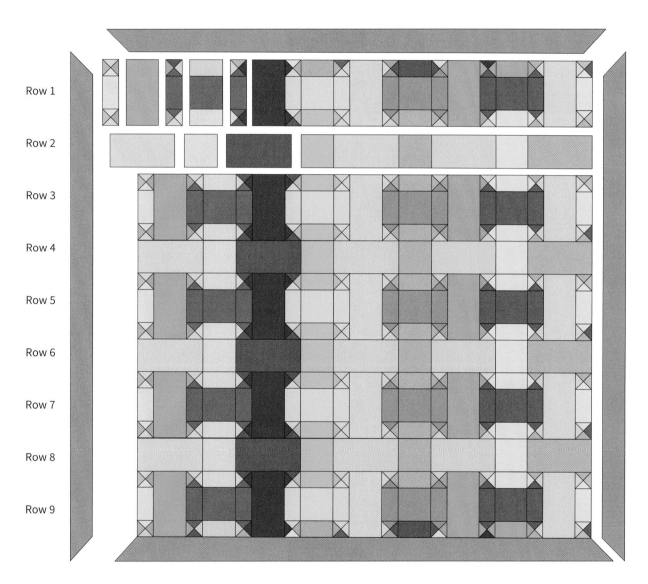

Row 1

Row 2

Row 3

Row 4

Row 5

Row 6

Row 7

Row 8

Row 9

Figure 8

COASTAL

Faded white and aqua fabrics with small-scale geometric and polka dot patterns make a light and airy quilt that reminds me of crystal-clear water and blue, blue sky. Keeping the colors in a very tight range helps to maintain a casual and classic look.

FARMHOUSE

You can add a little sweetness to your Farmhouse style by throwing in some pink with your red, green, and gray. This color palette is still classic but has a bit of an old-fashioned vibe, giving you the best of both worlds! With feedsack flower prints alongside tonal medallions, this quilt says farmhouse quite nicely.

MINIMAL ZEN

Linens and cottons in earth-tone taupe, brown, and cream make for a sparse quilt, yet with quite a bit of visual interest. Using "warm" neutral colors in your Minimal Zen decor can help to add a little coziness to a design style that can sometimes feel sterile and uninviting.

VINTAGE RETRO

Grab a bundle of 1930s reproduction fabrics and get stitching! Using pre-cut bundles are a fast and easy way to choose coordinating fabrics — and there are quite a few bundles and designs to choose from. The orange, green, and navy prints shown here are a fun departure from the standard pastel 1930s prints, and have such a fun retro vibe, perfect for your vintage bedroom.

Minimal Zen

BEADED CURTAIN

This design uses a single shape, a circle, to create a meditative feel. The fabrics you choose, of course, will make a big difference in creating a look you enjoy. Using large-scale printed fabrics will lessen the focus on the circles and place emphasis on the fabrics. If you use medium- to small-scale fabrics, especially tonal prints, the emphasis remains on the circles themselves.

Finished Quilt: 90 1/2" x 90 1/2"

Pieced by Sue Brandon and Susan Roy;
Quilted by April Rosenthal

MATERIALS

Fat Quarters (18" x 22"): 15

Background Fabric: 6½ yards

Backing Fabric: 8 ¼ yards 42"-wide, or 2¾ yards 108"-wide

Binding Fabric: ¾ yards

Batting: 97" x 97"

Compass or Die Cutter

CUTTING

My appliqué method is to use a fabric glue stick and stitch around the appliqué. When laundering, this glue washes out completely. You can also use a liquid fabric glue that must be ironed to set. Either way, glue basting is quick, easy, and leaves your quilt soft and flexible. If you prefer an alternate appliqué method, note that instructions do not indicate fusible webbing.

From 15 Fat Quarters, cut:
(5) 6½" circles (using a compass or die cutter) from each of 13 fat quarters
(6) circles from 2 fat quarters
You will have a total of 77 circles

From Background Fabric, cut:
(120) 7" squares
(5) 6½" x 40" strips
(2) 11½" x 40" strips
(2) 14½" x 40" strips

From Binding Fabric, cut:
(10) 2½" x 42" strips

APPLIQUÉ

Center and pin (or temporarily glue) each circle to the center of a 7" background square. Stitch around the outside of the circle using a zigzag stitch, blanket stitch, or other decorative stitch as desired. **(Fig. 1)**

PUTTING IT TOGETHER

1 Referencing Figure 2, lay out the squares as shown. Stitch blocks together into 10 rows of 12 blocks each. Press seams to the side, alternating the direction by row so that seams nest.

2 Pinning as needed, stitch rows together. Press the entire top.

3 Piece 14½" and 11½" strips as needed for the top and bottom borders. Attach and trim, then press toward border. Piece 6 ½" strips as needed for the side borders. Attach and trim, then press toward borders.

FINISHING

Layer, baste, quilt, and bind using your preferred methods.

TIP: I used a die cutter to create the circles for this quilt. If you do the same, depending on your machine, you may only get four circles from each fat quarter, so purchase fabric accordingly.

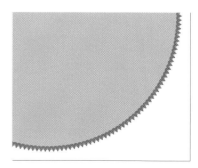

Figure 1

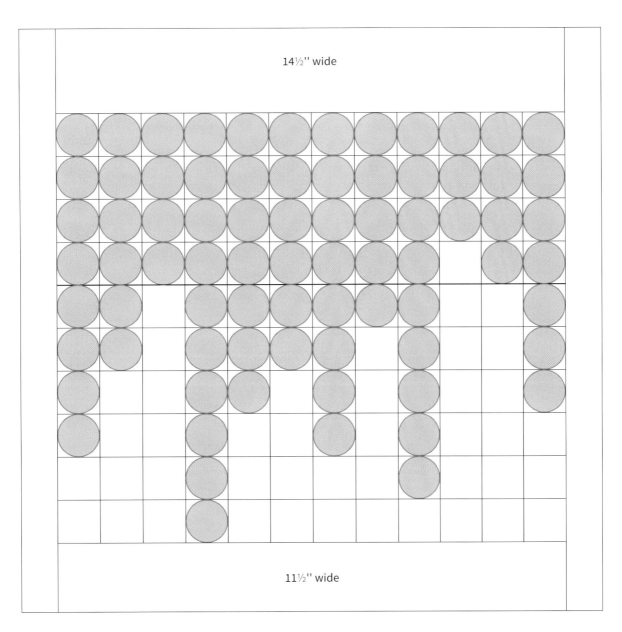

14½'' wide

11½'' wide

Figure 2

GLOBAL ECLECTIC

Bright, primitive, hand-stamped prints make the perfect global version of Beaded Curtain. Just like every city has its own color palette, each global quilt does, too. The trick to maintaining this style is to use bright colors, contrasting prints, and a non-solid background.

FARMHOUSE

Floral fabrics in reds, navies, and creams make for a feminine farmhouse quilt that has a wisp of nostalgia and patriotism. Many Farmhouse-style homes incorporate some type of red, white, and blue in their styling as a classic nod to their country. Of course, if these colors don't represent your homeland, substitute colors that do.

VINTAGE RETRO

Vintage printed bedsheets are one way to get a lot of retro charm into your quilt. You can often find these sheets at estate sales, flea markets, and secondhand shops. These prints make for a light and airy quilt that will bring an old-time springtime right into your bedroom.

COASTAL

Beads in fading shades of sea glass blue with just a few prints here and there are the perfect choice for this Coastal-style quilt. Simple, calm, and relaxing, these blues are sure to remind you of the ocean.

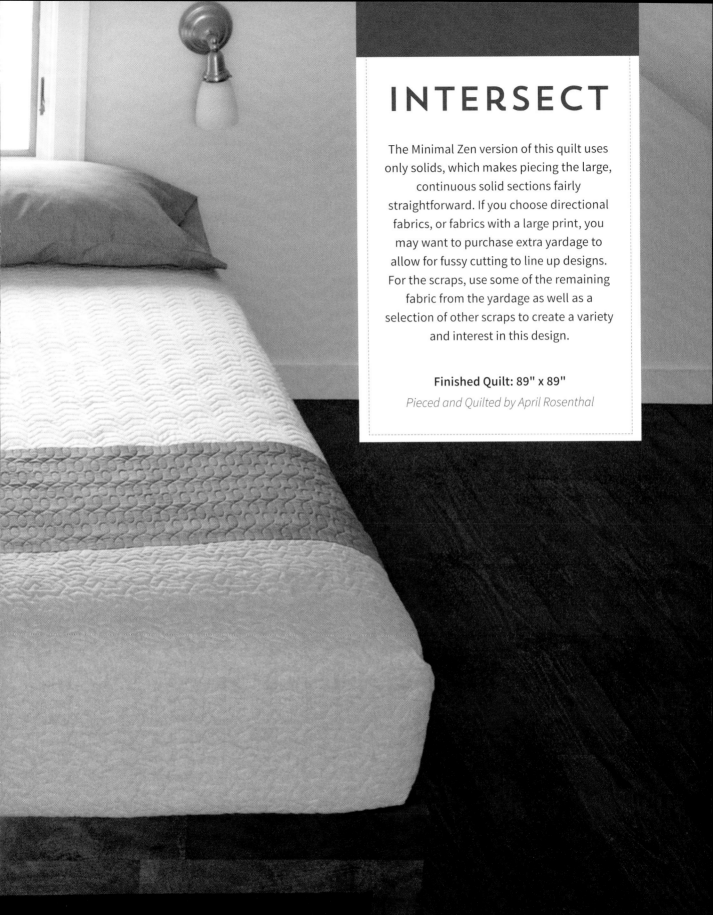

INTERSECT

The Minimal Zen version of this quilt uses only solids, which makes piecing the large, continuous solid sections fairly straightforward. If you choose directional fabrics, or fabrics with a large print, you may want to purchase extra yardage to allow for fussy cutting to line up designs. For the scraps, use some of the remaining fabric from the yardage as well as a selection of other scraps to create a variety and interest in this design.

Finished Quilt: 89" x 89"

Pieced and Quilted by April Rosenthal

MATERIALS

Panel A Fabric: ¾ yard

Panel B Fabric: 1 yard

Panel C Fabric: 3 yards or 1½ yards 108"-wide fabric

Panel D Fabric: ⅔ yard

Panel E Fabric: 1 yard

Panel F Fabric: ⅔ yard

Panel G Fabric: ½ yard

Panel H Fabric: 1⅓ yard

Patchwork Panel Scraps: Approximately ½ yard multi-colored solid scraps, each at least 2" square

Backing Fabric: 8 yards 42"-wide, or 2¾ yards 108"-wide

Binding Fabric: ¾ yards

Batting: 96" x 96"

TIP: When a quilt calls for large pieces, see if you can find a 108"-wide fabric that will fit your color scheme and design. Not only will this save you piecing time, but it will also save you money. This extra-wide fabric is typically more cost effective than buying the same yardage in standard widths.

CUTTING

From Panel A Fabric, cut:
(2) 11½" x 40" strips

From Panel B Fabric, cut:
(2) 17" x 40" strips

From Panel C Fabric, cut:
(2) 50" x 40" rectangles (40"-wide fabric), or (1) 50" x 61" rectangle (108"-wide fabric)

From Panel D Fabric, cut:
(1) 11½" x 17" rectangle

From Panel E Fabric, cut:
(2) 17" x 40" strips

From Panel F Fabric, cut:
(1) 11½" x 22½" rectangle

From Panel G Fabric, cut:
(1) 17" x 22½" rectangle

From Panel H Fabric, cut:
(2) 22½" x 40" strips

From Scraps, cut:
(81) 2" squares

From Binding Fabric, cut:
(10) 2½" x 42" strips

PIECING THE PATCHWORK SQUARE

TIP: When piecing lots of tiny squares, it's a good idea to use a scant seam allowance. A scant seam allowance is just slightly smaller than the called for measurement. I usually just adjust my needle one position closer to the edge of the fabric, and that does the job!

1 Using a scant ¼" seam, chain piece your 2" squares randomly into 27 sets of three. Press seams to one side.

2 Stitch the 2" square rows into nine-patch blocks, rotating the center set of blocks 180 degrees to allow seams to nest. Press seams to one side. **(Fig. 1)**

3 Stitch nine-patch blocks into 3 rows of 3 blocks, rotating and repressing seams if needed to nest seams. **(Fig. 2)**

4 Stitch nine-patch rows together, pressing seams to one side. Finished block should measure 17" square. **(Fig. 3)**

5 Set aside.

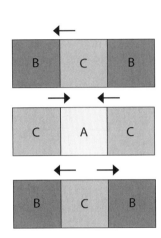

Figure 1

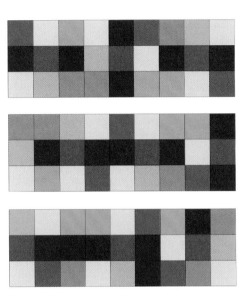

Figure 2

Figure 3

PIECING PANELS

1 Piece together the remaining sections as follows:

Panel A
Stitch rectangles together on the short edge. Press seam open. Measure and trim to 11 ½" x 50".

Panel B
Stitch rectangles together on the short edge. Press seam open. Measure and trim to 17" x 50".

Panel C
If you are using 108"-wide fabric for this section, skip to Section E. If you are using 40"-wide fabric for this section, stitch pieces together on the 50" side. Press seam open. Measure and trim to 50" x 61".

Panel E
Stitch rectangles together on the short edge. Press seam open. Measure and trim to 17" x 61".

Panel H
Stitch rectangles together on the short edge. Press seam open. Measure and trim to 22½" x 61".

PUTTING IT TOGETHER

1 Sew the first row by stitching together the long sides of Panels A and B. Sew Panel C to Panel B. Press both seams toward Panel B.

2 Sew the second segment by stitching Panel D to the left side of Patchwork Square. Press toward Panel D. Sew Panel E to the right side of Patchwork Square. Press toward Panel E.

3 Sew the third segment by stitching Panel F to the left side of Panel G, and Panel H to the right side of Panel G. Press both seams toward Panel G.

4 Pin Row 1 to Row 2 at both ends, in the center, and every 3" along the length of the seam. Nest seams at the intersection between panels. Stitch. Press toward top piece.

5 Pin Row 2 to Row 3 at both ends, in the center, and every 3" along the length of the seam. Nest seams at the intersection between panels. Stitch. Press toward bottom piece. (Fig. 4)

FINISHING
Layer, baste, quilt, and bind using your preferred methods.

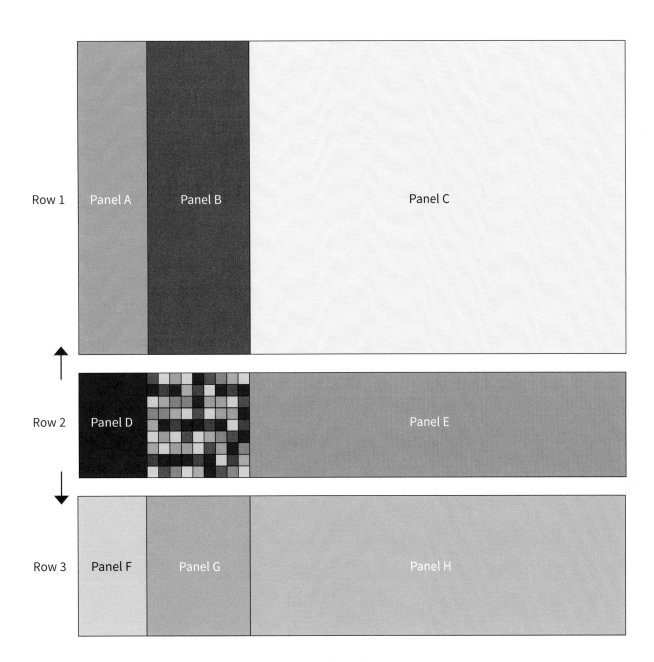

Row 1

Panel A

Panel B

Panel C

Row 2

Panel D

Panel E

Row 3

Panel F

Panel G

Panel H

Figure 4

GLOBAL ECLECTIC

Eclectic, saturated, ornate prints combine to make a very busy intersection! The combination of fiery red, copper, brown, and yellow with a splash of bold teal makes an exotic statment that reminds me of a sunset on an unfamiliar coast.

FARMHOUSE

Dusty calicos and small-scale prints in classic colors combine to create a perfectly Farmhouse version of an otherwise modern quilt. Contrasting the modern pattern with the more traditional fabric is a delightful surprise that is fresh and lovely to look at.

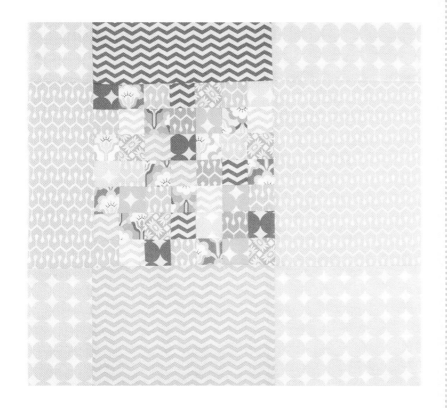

VINTAGE RETRO

Light, sorbet colors in updated florals and geometric prints make for a modern vintage quilt that is sure to please the eye. When using prints that have a medium- to large-scale design, remember to break them up with smaller prints or solids so that the quilt doesn't get too busy; you don't want to lose the design in the piecing.

COASTAL

Keeping most of the quilt in varying shades of white with an intersection of aquas makes a stunning but simple statement. This Coastal version of Intersect conjures the feel of white sand beaches and small glass treasures sparkling in the sunlight.

Vintage Retro

PRIZED POSIES

I've always loved the look of traditional Dresden plate blocks, but always wished there was a way to make them without the appliqué in the center. I decided to paper piece these Posies, and problem solved! The result is a beautiful quilt full of blooms that would win top prize at any county fair.

Finished Quilt: 88" x 88"

Finished Block Size: 14" x 14"

Pieced by Gaylene Rosenthal and April Rosenthal; Quilted by April Rosenthal

MATERIALS

Fat Quarters (18'' x 22''): 30

Background Fabric: 4 ¼ yards

Inner Border Fabric: ⅔ yard

Outer Border Fabric: 2 yards

Backing Fabric: 8 yards 42'' wide-or 2 ¾ yards 108''-wide

Binding Fabric: ¾ yards

Batting: 94'' x 94''

CUTTING

From each of 30 Fat Quarters, cut:
(10) 4'' x 8'' rectangles (A1, B1, C1)

From Background Fabric, cut:
(100) 3'' x 5'' rectangles (B3)

(100) 2¾'' squares (B2)

(200) 1¾'' x 3'' rectangles (A2, C2)

(200) 2¾'' x 3¼'' rectangles (A3, C3)

From Inner Border Fabric, cut:
(8) 3'' x 40'' strips

From Outer Border Fabric, cut:
(10) 7'' x 40'' strips

From Binding Fabric, cut:
(10) 2½'' x 42'' strips

PREPARATION

Make 100 copies of the paper piecing templates (see facing page). Use thin copy paper. Roughly cut out each template piece, leaving the seam allowance around each one. You should have a total of 100 of each template, A, B, and C.

The block is divided into 12 simple paper pieced sections. Each block has 4 each of sections A, B, and C. If you are new to paper piecing, see the instructions on page 84. If not, follow the directions below.

1 Shorten stitch length to 1.5 and begin paper piecing all printed templates, using cut pieces for the sections referred to in the cutting instructions. For example, the 4'' x 8'' rectangles cut from fat quarters are used for all A1, B1, and C1 sections.

2 Leave paper on blocks. Continue until you have pieced 100 of each section. Trim excess fabric around edges to seam allowance line on paper templates. **(Fig. 1)**

TIP: Paper piecing is such a fun technique and a great way to make accurate blocks without templates. Remember to use thin paper when paper piecing so that it tears away easily when you no longer need it.

PUTTING IT TOGETHER

1 Make quarter blocks by stitching one of each section together. Section B in the middle, section A to the right, and section C to the left. Press seams open.

TIP: Pressing seams open distributes bulk and helps the block lie more flat. Use lots of steam and a little starch to get seams to press open well.

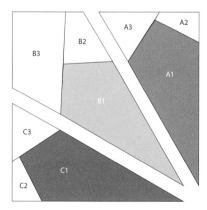

Figure 1

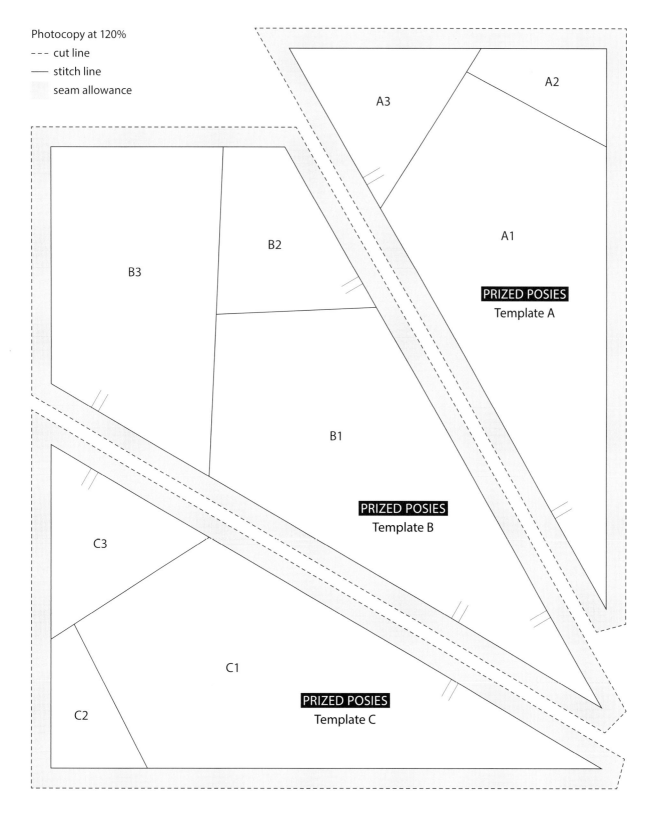

Photocopy at 120%
- - - cut line
——— stitch line
▨ seam allowance

A3

A2

A1

PRIZED POSIES
Template A

B2

B3

B1

PRIZED POSIES
Template B

C3

C1

C2

PRIZED POSIES
Template C

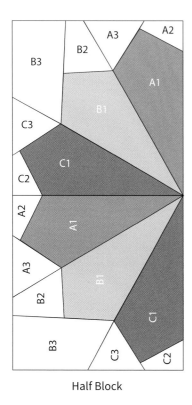

Half Block

Full Block

Figure 2

2 Piece quarter blocks together to make 23 full blocks and 4 half blocks. (**Fig. 2**)

3 Lay out blocks in 5 rows, beginning and ending rows 2 and 4 with half blocks. Piece blocks into rows, pressing seams to the side. Refer to the quilt diagram for placement.

4 Piece rows together, matching intersections and pinning at ends, center, and every 3" along the length.

5 For the inner border, piece 3" yellow border strips together as needed. Attach and trim, then press toward border. For the outer border, piece 7" gray border strips together as needed. Attach and trim, then press toward border. (**Fig. 3**)

FINISHING

Gently remove paper from the back of all blocks. Layer, baste, quilt, and bind using your preferred methods.

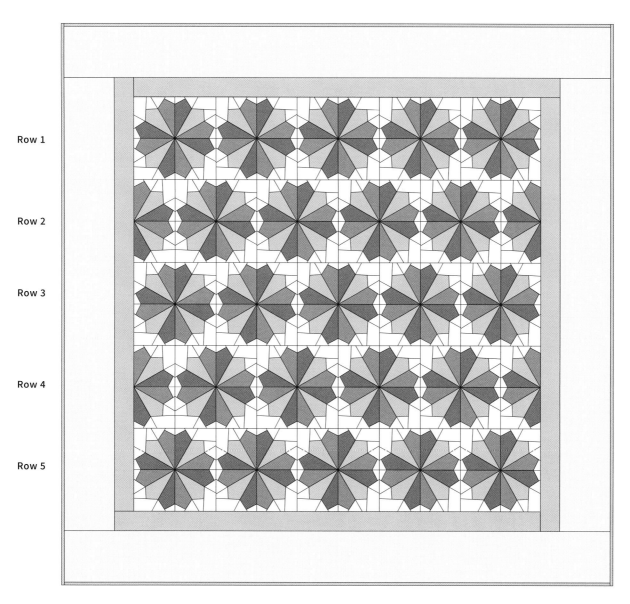

Row 1

Row 2

Row 3

Row 4

Row 5

Figure 3

PAPER PIECING

Paper foundation piecing, commonly called paper piecing, is a method of piecing quilt blocks using a printed paper for stitch lines. It allows a sewist to make blocks with precise or complex angles that would be difficult to cut and piece otherwise.

When paper piecing, you will need a printed paper foundation for each block or piece of a block. In the case of both Prized Posies and Kansas, you will need 100 copies of each block unit.

Here are a few things you'll want to remember: The printed side of the paper is the "stitching side." This means that anytime you sew pieces together, you'll be doing it with the printed side of the paper facing up and your fabric facing down. Your fabric is always placed on the unprinted side. The numbers on the paper refer to the order in which you will sew the pieces together. The lines on the paper are where you will sew.

To get started paper piecing, cut out the foundation templates (see pages 81 and 91) just outside the seam allowance edge. With the printed side of the paper foundation facing you, place the appropriate piece of fabric — with the wrong side of the fabric facing the unmarked side of the paper — over the area on the foundation that is marked as the first piece (A1, B1, etc.). You may need to hold the paper up to a window or light in order to place

Figure 1

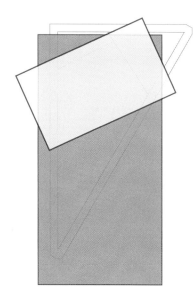

Figure 2

the fabric correctly. Make sure the edges of the fabric piece extend at least ¼" beyond the stitching lines of the area. It's okay if the fabric is significantly bigger than the area you are covering. You can trim away excess later. Pin or glue the piece in place, avoiding the stitching lines. (Fig. 1)

Choose a piece of fabric that is the correct size to cover the second piece (A2, B2, etc.) generously, extending at least 1/4" or more past the stitching lines. Place it right sides together with the first piece, aligning it so that it is appropriately positioned to be stitched on the stitching line between pieces 1 and

2. Pin the second piece in place, avoiding the stitching line. (Fig. 2)

Flip over the paper so that the stitching side (printed side) is   facing up. Stitch on the line between pieces 1 and 2, starting a few stitches before the line begins and ending a few stitches beyond. Trim threads. (Fig. 3)

Flip over the paper and open the seam you just stitched, making sure your second piece covers the entire second area accurately, extending beyond the sewing lines at least ¼". If it doesn't, carefully unpick the seam and reposition. If it does, close the pieced seam, fold back the paper foundation, and trim

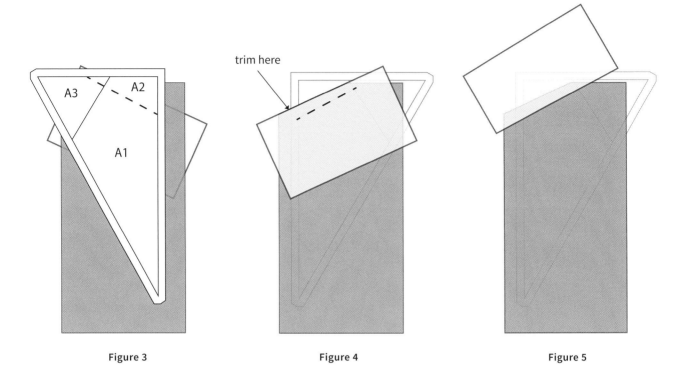

A3 A2 A1

trim here

Figure 3   Figure 4   Figure 5

seam allowance to¼". Be careful to avoid cutting the foundation paper. (Fig. 4)

Reopen the seam and press in place with a dry iron — no steam. Steam will curl your paper and make it harder to work with. (Fig. 5)

Continue piecing this way to finish each block unit. Keep in mind that any piece that is at the outside of the block should cover well past the ¼" seam allowance marked on the foundation piece. It will be trimmed when the block or unit is complete.

When the block or unit is complete, you may choose to use a very long stitch length to baste around the edges of your block, particularly where there are seams that intersect the outside edge. This will help reinforce weak areas or bias edges.

Trim the block or unit to the seam allowance lines by placing the block paper side up on a rotary mat and trimming on the ¼" seam allowance line. Be careful not to let the ruler slip on the paper. Paper should not be removed if the block will be sewn to other paper pieced blocks. Once blocks or units are stitched together, carefully remove paper. You may find a small pair of tweezers to be helpful when removing small pieces of paper from intersections.

make it your style

GLOBAL ECLECTIC

Polka dot linens and designs in vibrant colors combine to make a multi-textured (and very fun!) version of this quilt. When you're choosing fabrics for your quilt, consider including substrates like linen, flannel, velveteen, or voile to add depth and texture.

FARMHOUSE

A hallmark of classic farmhouses is linens that change with the holidays. Traditional Christmas prints in rich colors are the perfect choice for this quilt, and remind me of brisk winters and baking sugar cookies while the snow falls on the quiet fields outside.

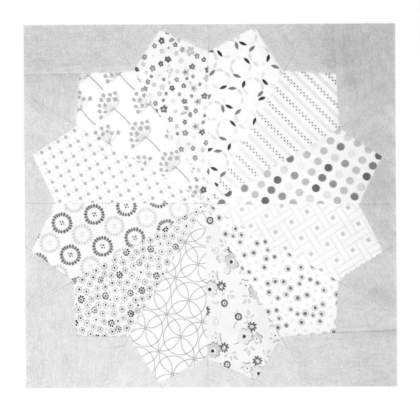

MINIMAL ZEN

With a gray background made from shot cotton and blossoms from a combination of various white background prints, this minimal interpretation combines visual interest and simplicity. Keeping the background consistent and the prints small in scale allows the quilt to remain minimal even while using many fabrics.

COASTAL

A bold and nautical navy and white quilt always makes me think of crisp khakis and white summer sundresses. Keeping the colors simple allowed me to use a few novelty prints without the quilt becoming too busy or kitschy.

KANSAS

I had so much fun combining fabrics in each block of this quilt, keeping the aquas and limes together, the reds and oranges in the middle sections, and the greys in the outer tips. I did my best to use as many fabrics as I could without distracting from the design. Using various background fabrics also lends to the vintage feel.

Finished Quilt: 89" x 89"

Finished Block Size: 15" x 15"

Pieced and Quilted by April Rosenthal

MATERIALS

Fabrics A1, A5, A6:
Approximately 4 yards

Fabric A2: Approximately
2 yards

Fabric A3: Approximately
1¼ yards

Fabric A4: Approximately
¾ yard

Sashing and Border Fabric:
2½ yards

Backing Fabric: 8 yards 42"-
wide or 2¾ yards 108"-wide

Binding Fabric: ¾ yards dark
print fabric for binding

Batting: 95" x 95"

*Note: All Materials are
approximate due to the use
of scraps

TIP: If you're using lots of
different background fabrics
like I did, consider doing
the same with your sashing
strips. This will help maintain the scrappy look of the
quilt and help you use up
the scraps in your stash.

CUTTING

From Fabric A1, cut:
(50) 5" squares

Subcut once on the diagonal to
make 100 triangles

From Fabric A2, cut:
(100) 3 ¼" x 6½" rectangles

From Fabric A3, cut: (100) 3 ¼" x
4¼" rectangles

From Fabric A4, cut:
(100) 2 ¼" x 3 ½" rectangles

From Fabric A5, A6, cut:
(100) 5" x 9" rectangles

Subcut once on the diagonal to
make 200 triangles

From Sashing and Border
Fabric, cut:
(20) 1½" x 15½" strips

(8) 1½" x 42" strips

(10) 5½" x 40" strips

From Binding Fabric, cut:
(10) 2½" x 42" strips

PREPARATION

Make 100 copies of the paper
piecing template (see facing page).
Use thin copy paper. Roughly cut
out the template pieces, leaving the
seam allowance around each.

PAPER PIECING

See page 84 for instructions on
paper piecing.

1 The Kansas block is made using
4 of the same paper pieced sections. Shorten stitch length to 1.5
and begin paper piecing all printed
templates, using cut pieces for the
sections referred to in the cutting
instructions. For example, the 2¼" x
3½" rectangles cut from dark-toned
fabrics are used for all A4 sections.
Leave paper on quarter blocks.

2 Continue until you have pieced
100 quarter blocks. Trim excess
fabric around edges to seam
allowance line on paper templates.

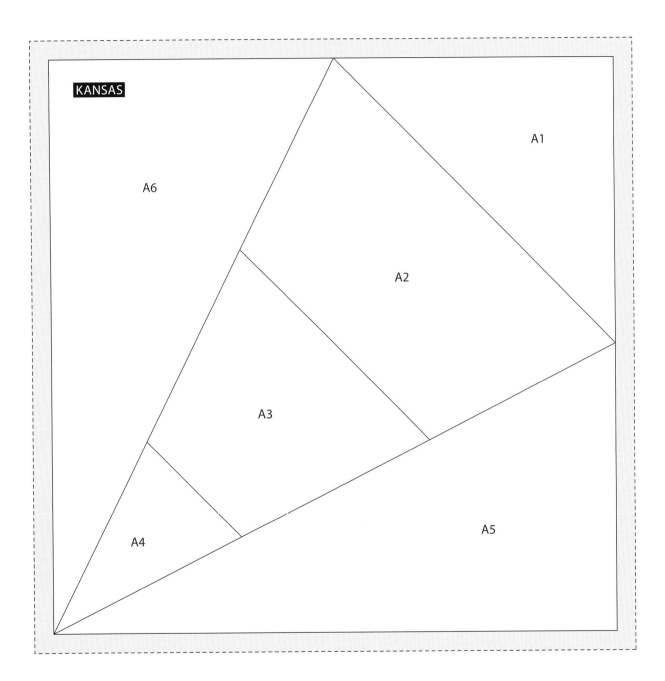

KANSAS

A1

A6

A2

A3

A4

A5

Photocopy at 125%

- - - cut line

—— stitch line

▨ seam allowance

PUTTING IT TOGETHER

1 Piece together four quarter blocks to make one full block. Press seams open (**Fig. 1**). Repeat to create a total of 25 full blocks.

2 Referencing Figure 2, arrange blocks in 5 rows. Place a 1½" x 15½" sashing strip between each block. Piece blocks and sashing into rows. Press seams toward sashing strips.

3 Piece together (2) 1½" x 42" sashing strips to make one long piece of sashing. Repeat with the 6 remaining 40" sashing strips. Piece rows of blocks together with sashing between each row. Pin at ends, center, and every 3" along the length. Press toward sashing. Trim edges of sashing as necessary to square up your quilt top.

4 For the border, piece 5½" strips together as needed. Attach and trim, then press toward border adding the top and bottom borders first. Repeat for the sides. (**Fig. 2**)

FINISHING

Gently remove the paper from the backs of the blocks. Layer, baste, quilt, and bind using your preferred methods.

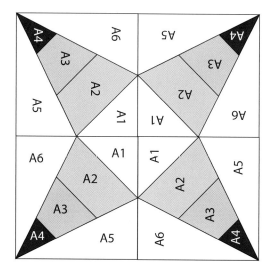

Figure 1

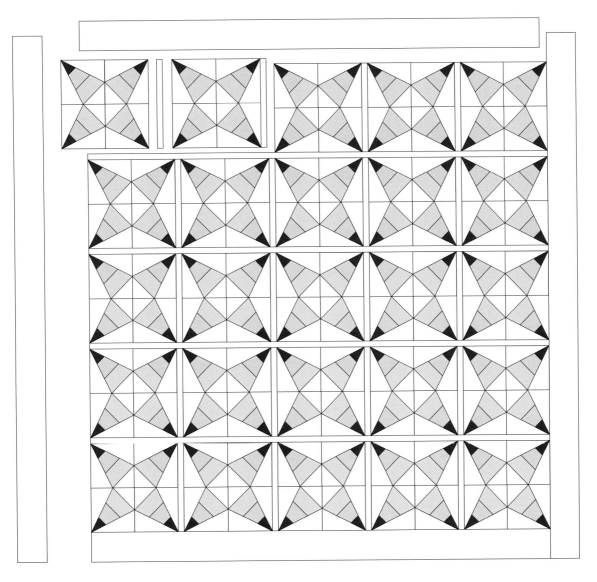

Figure 2

GLOBAL ECLECTIC

If you're drawn to drama, you may want to add one or two deep colors to your quilt to up the contrast and create an instant mood. Here, I added dark navy and violet to red, gold, aqua, and kumquat orange for an eclectic quilt.

FARMHOUSE

If you'd like to go a little unconventional but still keep a Farmhouse feel, use familiar prints like polka dots, medium florals, and stripes in colors that aren't quite so traditional. In this case, I used prints in purples, teals, and golds — but retained the traditional feel by keeping the print motifs simple and classic.

MINIMAL ZEN

Sometimes a little red is all it takes. In this quilt, gray and black are accented with a few shots of vibrant red to create a focal point that can't be ignored. Keep your palette restrained to only one vibrant color at a time to really bring focus and a Minimal Zen simplicity to your design.

COASTAL

The first time I went on a cruise, I just kept taking pictures of the water. I was fascinated by the constantly changing colors of the Caribbean seas — from a seaweed green to a clear vibrant aqua and everything in between. This Coastal-style version of Kansas is a nod to my tropical memories of that first cruise.

FINISHING TOUCHES

How you finish a quilt is just as important as the design, the blocks, the fabrics, and the colors that go into a quilt top. Your finishing touches can elevate a simple piece of patchwork to an heirloom, even a masterpiece.

There are only a few steps to finishing a quilt, and each provides plenty of opportunities not only to personalize your quilt even further, but to customize it to be the perfect item for your bed, climate, and personality.

First, we will discuss choosing backing fabric. Though using a quilting cotton is by far the most common approach to backing a quilt, there are many other materials available — many of which might be better suited to your tastes. We will also discuss a quick and economical way to speed up backing a large quilt — that doesn't involve piecing!

Next, I will talk you through the myriad options of batting for your quilt, and why you might want to consider something different than your batting standby. With dozens of batting choices out there, from soy to wool, and rayon to silk, it's worth exploring the options. In addition, we'll talk about the "warmness" of each batting, how each batting breathes, shrinks, and washes.

Another way to add your personal stamp to a quilt is how you quilt it. I will tell you a little bit about the merits of hand quilting, and some about why machine quilting might be the best option to choose.

Of course, no quilt is complete without that last personal touch. Perhaps you want to include a custom quilt label (you should!), some hand embroidery, or a monogram? No problem. I've got you covered. I will talk about ways to add the perfect custom touch to your already beautiful quilt.

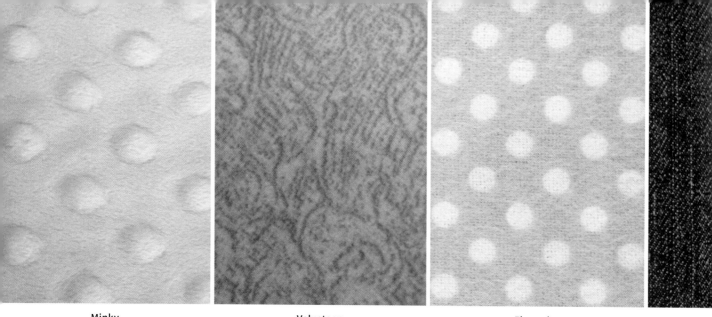

Minky · Velveteen · Flannel · Denim

Backing

Choosing the perfect backing fabric is one of the most important parts of quilt making — after all, it is the back of the quilt that will touch your skin! Below, I will detail seven backing options, and the reasons you might want to use them.

MINKY

A classic backing fabric for juvenile and baby quilts, minky is used for our sweetest and most gentle little ones for one reason: it is unbelievably soft. It is usually made from 100% polyester, and because of this, it is generally not going to breathe well — which for some people means that it might make you sweat. Polyester fabrics retain body heat and are considered a "warm" fabric. I personally use minky on the back of quilts that will be used in the cold Utah winter, because with a minky backing, the quilt is heavy, warm, super soft, and drapes well. Minky is a great choice for a warm winter quilt — especially if you tend to feel cold at night.

VELVETEEN

The grown-up's minky, velveteen, can be used when you want a luxurious but still very soft quilt back. It is made from cotton, and has a short pile of threads that come up from the surface of the fabric. These threads are usually pressed flat — which means that the fabric has what's called a "nap," or a directional texture. Velveteen drapes well, has a medium weight, and is more breathable than polyester. It often feels cool to the touch, but warms up with contact. Velveteen typically has a sleek, smooth feel when touched in the direction of the fibers.

FLANNEL

If you're looking for a fabric that is warm and still breathes well, flannel is your answer. A quilt backed in flannel is a great option if you want a warm, mid-weight quilt that won't make you sweat. Flannel is usually 100% brushed cotton, and can even be found in organic varieties. An advantage to using flannel is that many fabric designers now release flannels at the same time and in the same pattern or color family as their quilting cottons, so you could choose a coordinating print to back your quilt. Think of using flannel for a lightweight winter quilt, or as a good backing for spring and fall quilts.

Linen   Cotton Voile   Quilting Cotton

TWILL, DENIM, + CHAMBRAY

Heavy duty and a little stiff, twill, denim, or chambray can be a good choice for a quilt backing when you need something durable, able to block drafts, or want a rustic feel. Made from cotton, these fabrics contains thicker individual threads than lighter-weight quilting cottons; because of this, they wear well and have quite a bit of weight but won't bunch under you as you sleep. If you back your quilt with one of these heavy fabrics and are using a longarmer to do the quilting, check on their guidelines for heavy fabrics.

LINEN

Crisp and cool, linen is a great choice for lightweight summer quilts. Linen is highly breathable and exceptionally suited for warm and humid climates; it absorbs moisture easily, and also dries quickly. Linen actually becomes stronger when wet so remains un-damaged through many washings. If you have skin or allergy issues, linen is a good choice because it is naturally microbe resistant and does not lint. Linen can feel slightly stiff when new but becomes softer with washing and use. For a durable quilt backing that will keep you cool in the summer, linen is your new best friend.

COTTON VOILE

Lightweight and wonderfully smooth, cotton voile is the lightest of the backing fabrics discussed here. Cotton voile is cool to the touch; it has a luxurious, satin-like feel and a beautiful sheen. It is thin, however, and can damage easily. Some voiles are so thin that they are almost transparent. If you choose to use cotton voile for your quilt backing, look for voiles made by quilt fabric manufacturers, exclusively sold at independent fabric shops. I have found these to be a little more durable and slightly thicker than standard voiles, and opaque enough to work well — with the added advantage of having designs that often match popular quilting cotton fabric lines. Most manufacturers suggest washing cotton voile on delicate, and line drying — which works just fine for a summer quilt.

QUILTING COTTON

The most common choice for backing, quilting cotton is a light yet durable fabric that is a good option for all-purpose quilts, or for use in temperate climates. An additional benefit to using quilting cotton is the availability of 108"-wide yardage, which typically costs only 10% more than standard width — for more than double the fabric. Of course, the best part of using 108"-wide yardage is that you don't need to piece your quilt back — you can simply buy as much length as you need, and get quilting!

Batting

I'll be honest: the first time I saw a batting display with dozens of options and words I wasn't familiar with (scrim, bonded, hand, drape), I was overwhelmed. After trying (in vain) to figure out which batting was the "best" choice, I finally ended up searching the internet for "which batting should I use for my quilt," and went with the answer from the blog that I liked the design of best. My method wasn't very scientific, or well informed.

Luckily, that blog suggested a natural cotton batting — one of the most popular and universal battings available. I continued to use cotton until I got my own longarm and started experimenting with battings for different lofts, less warping and stretching, and trying to avoid bearding (that's when the batting fibers come through your fabric and make it look hairy or fuzzy). I see that I had put myself at a disadvantage by not exploring the other options.

Manufacturers are constantly developing new materials and ways to make their products. Keep an eye out for flax, corn, alpaca, even batting made from recycled bottles. There are a lot of options and advantages to each type of batting. Give them a chance and see which is the perfect choice for you!

COTTON

Cotton is a natural fiber, breathes well, and is a comfortable batting for most climates. It has a low loft (height), but is fairly dense — even heavy. Cotton batting typically shrinks from 3% to 5% when washed and dried in hot temperatures, which contributes to the "crinkly" look that a lot of quilters love. It comes in many varieties, including bleached white, natural, and even black. In addition, you can purchase cotton batting with or without "scrim," which is a lightweight layer of polypropylene that adds stability. This is useful to avoic stretching, pulling, or shifting. Scrim will add a almost unnoticable amount of stiffness to your quilt.

WOOL

Wool batting is a sustainable, renewable, and natural fiber. It is harvested from sheep by shearing, like a haircut. It does not harm the sheep, and like hair, it grows back. Wool is extremely soft, breathable, and light. Wool is considered to be the warmest batting available, but it also stays cool in the summer. Often, wool batting has been pre-washed and pre-shrunk (check your packaging) and so shrinks very little (2%), if at all. Many wool battings can be washed like any other batting. Wool batting holds its loft and bounces back into shape well; it doesn't hold creases and emphasizes both hand and machine quilting. Because wool is less dense, it is also a desirable batting for hand quilting.

SOY

According to one batting manufacturer, "Soy is the softest batting there is!" There is also the benefit of soy being a natural fiber. Many consider it a "green" batting option, because soy is reneable and sustainable. It breathes, absorbs moisture, and dries quickly. It is often found in a blend with cotton fibers; however, it is significantly thinner (lower loft) than cotton batting. Soy shrinks less than cotton and can be used for light-weight summer quilts. Because it is so thin, soy batting is easy to quilt by machine or hand.

BAMBOO

Like soy batting, bamboo batting is made from a sustainable, renewable source. It is soft, biodegradable, hypoallergenic, and naturally anti-bacterial. Bamboo batting has the same loft as cotton batting, without as much shrinkage. Bamboo batting contains a scrim, and is almost always found in a blend with cotton. Bamboo is a good choice for warm and/or humid climates, or if you want a mid-weight batting that is softer than cotton but still breathable. Bamboo is easily hand or machine quilted.

SILK

Silk batting is extremely soft, drapes very well, and is easily quilted. It is also more expensive than most batting types, except perhaps wool. Silk batting has medium warmth, but a very light weight. It shrinks up to 5% when washed, and it breathes well. Quilts made with silk batting typically must be hand washed and laid flat to dry. Due to this, silk batting would be best used in a summer quilt or in warm climates. Silk batting is not a good candidate for tied quilts.

POLYESTER

Polyester is a synthetic fiber. Because it is man-made, it comes in a variety of lofts, ranging from $1/16$" all the way up to 1" or more. The warmth of a polyester batting depends on the loft — the higher the loft, the warmer the quilt. Polyester is easily washable and does not shrink. It is more "puffy" than most quilt battings, and thus will help machine or hand quilting stand out. It is less breathable than natural fibers but generally more lightweight. If a high loft batting ($1/2$" or more) is used, the quilt will have a bit of stiffness, and is often tied.

COTTON-POLYESTER BLEND

A cotton-poly blend is typically 80% cotton and 20% polyester or a 50/50 mix of both fibers. The advantage to using this type of batting is that the polyester contributes strength and loft, while the cotton contributes breathability and softness. A cotton-poly blend batting shrinks less than all-cotton but more than all-polyester. It is a good choice for an all-season quilt or one that will be washed frequently. If you want batting that has the crinkliness of cotton and the loft of polyester, cotton-poly is for you.

Personal touches

There are so many ways to make a quilt your own. We've discussed design, fabric choices, styles, backing fabrics, and batting. There are also little touches you can include that really make the quilt a reflection of where you've been and who you are.

MONOGRAM

Perhaps just a name, or maybe you've recently married and want to celebrate that union. You could choose to omit a block from your quilt design and replace it with a monogrammed name, initial, or even "A + J." Monograms add a stately and upscale look and of course, make them very personal.

EMBROIDERY

Embroidery may be the perfect way to add a personal touch to your quilt. When I was a little girl, I had a quilt that I dragged along everywhere with me. My grandma had embroidered in the corner: "To baby, Love Grandma Kirby" with a little heart and flower. This tiny little touch made me feel loved and remembered. Perhaps there is a word, phrase, or message you would like to remember, or a small emblem that is significant to you: a small bird, a religious symbol, a character in another language. These are all beautiful options for personalizing quilts and linens. To get your ideas flowing, I have included ten embroidery motifs in this book (page 108) that go along with the five styles.

CUSTOM QUILTING

You might choose to have your longarm quilter actually write the words to your favorite poem, lyrics, scripture, or mantra in thread. I once saw a quilt that had the words of a couple's wedding vows quilted into it. I wrote "secret messages" to my nieces and nephews in the quilting of their quilts. Something simple and just for them. I am a big believer in the power of words and thoughts.

TRIMS

If you enjoy vintage trims — lace, rickrack, pom-poms, and ribbons — you may opt to use those trims in your quilt. A simple and attractive way to use them would be to stitch them on as you place your binding, letting them peek out from the binding on the front side of your quilt. Another option would be to add them as trim to a pillowcase or sheet (see page 114). Instead of these lovely trims gathering dust somewhere where you rarely see them, put them to good use and enjoy them day after day. Please note, adding vintage trims to your quilt may require that you be more careful in the washing process.

COLOR

Add a splash of color that is significant to you. For example, when I told my husband I wanted to make him a "nap quilt," I asked him which colors he would like me to use. He surprised me when along with his favorite browns and greens he suggested a bit of pink, orange, and blue. I must have looked very confused because he continued to explain: he wanted a quilt made from the colors he liked, but wanted me to add in a little bit of pink to represent our daughter, Lily, a bit of blue for our son, Beckham, and some orange to signify me. Our favorite colors in his quilt (see page 108) remind him of us every time he uses it.

LABEL

A final personal touch you might add is a label. Typically this is a piece of fabric pieced into or appliquéd onto the quilt back that has information about who pieced the quilt, when it was made, and any other relevant details. A quilt label is a good idea not only for writing a To/From message if your quilt is a gift, but also for historical and record-keeping purposes.

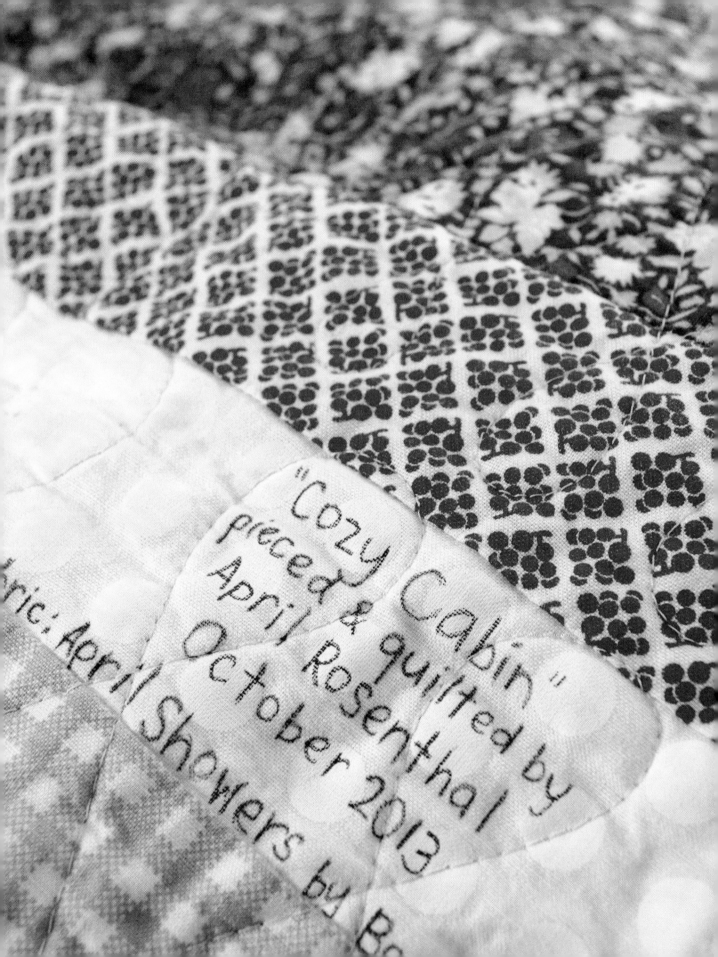

"Cozy Cabin"
pieced & quilted by
April Rosenthal
October 2013

Fabric: April Showers by Bo

Hand quilting vs. Machine quilting

Another way to customize your quilt is how you choose to quilt it. While whole books can be (and have been!) written on the merits, techniques, and advantages of any given method, I feel that both hand quilting and machine quilting are beautiful depending on the look and feel you're going for.

DENSITY

How densely your quilt is quilted, whether by hand or machine, will make a big difference in the final look, feel, and drape.

Loosely quilted with quilting spaced at least 5" apart can result in a more floppy and casual-looking. Because the quilting isn't securing the fabric in many places, it can bunch, shift, and wrinkle. Like a duvet cover, a quilt with very loose quilting (or a tied quilt) can separate between the layers and shift.

Standard density with quilting spaced ½" to 4" apart will usually give quilts a nice texture, keep together well, and won't shift or bunch. The tighter the quilting, the more "crinkly" it will be if it shrinks when washed. These quilts have a nice drape, and hold their shape well.

Heavily quilted with quilting spaced less than ½" apart tend to make quilts stiff and can actually be less warm than their more loosely quilted counterparts. Some batting, such as polyester, retains heat by trapping it between fibers. If the batting is smashed closely together with heavy quilting, the ability of

the fibers to retain heat is lessened. In addition, densely quilted quilts do not drape well, and will make a sort of tent to sleep under. They will not mold to body contours effectively. Some say that heavily quilted quilts become softer and more pliable over time, but I have not found that to be the case with my quilts.

HAND QUILTING

Beautiful, traditional, and custom are the words that come to mind when I think of hand quilting. With a long heritage and many, many skilled hands participating, hand quilting is still alive and well. Hand quilting is literally using a needle and thread to stitch the layers of your quilt together by hand. This can be done using hand quilting thread, which is thin but very strong, or using perle cotton or other twisted fibers, which are thicker and often vibrantly colored.

Just as there are many opinions about fabrics, battings, and threads, there are opinions from hand quilters about needles, techniques, and stitch lengths. If you have never tried hand quilting, many regional quilt guilds and local quilt shops

have resources and supplies, and often you will also find skilled and experienced hand quilters there who would love to pass on their passion to you. There are also many resources and tutorials online.

Hand quilting provides the opportunity to truly complete a quilt start to finish, to make design choices in regards to how the quilt is quilted, and to add accents and personality through those colors and designs. Hand quilting can be relaxing, even meditative. With practice, hand quilting can be precise and exact. Of course, this method takes more time and effort than just sending your quilt off to be quilted by machine, or even machine quilting it yourself.

Hand quilting contributes an amazing, heirloom quality to quilts. If a thicker thread is used, it can add a more primitive or playful feeling to the quilt, while a thin thread and small stitches can truly elevate a quilt from lovely to phenomenal. As with any handwork, use care and caution in laundering hand-quilted quilts; avoid machine washing or agitation.

MACHINE QUILTING

Whether you choose to machine quilt it yourself, or have it done by a longarm quilter, there are many things to consider when finishing your quilt by machine.

Machine quilting is a faster method than hand quilting; however, it can still take significant time if you do it yourself. In addition, you will need a large space to both baste and quilt your quilt. If you choose to machine quilt it yourself, remember that most sewing machines cannot accommodate a quilt larger than twin-size. There just isn't enough throat space. If you happen to have a very large domestic machine, this may not be a problem for you.

Though there are some people who are quite adept at moving their quilt under their machine, most machine-quilted quilts have an element of unsteadiness — a little bump in a straight line here, a lopsided flower there. These can be improved with practice, but because of the nature of free-motion quilting, they are almost never entirely eliminated — especially in larger quilts, which drag more. For most people, this is a part of the process, and they are happy with their finished product. If you, however, will be bothered by it, you may want to consider a computerized pattern done by a professional longarmer.

When you take your quilt to a professional longarm quilter, you will often have the choice between computerized quilting and custom quilting. Computerized quilting is typically the most economical option, but is the least design-oriented. Usually you will choose one design, and it will be stitched edge-to-edge on your entire quilt. This creates a consistent texture and look for the quilting, but will not highlight any specific element in your piecing. Computerized quilting is a good option for someone who doesn't want any inconsistencies in the quilting, or doesn't mind having the quilt quilted the same way all over.

If you choose to have a longarm quilter do custom quilting for you, be sure to tell her or him any "vision" you have for the quilting. There are many, many options for quilting designs — and they run the gamut from extremely traditional to extremely modern. Be aware of the look you like, and ask for suggestions. Longarm quilters can't read your mind, and they won't know what you want if you don't tell them. Most longarm quilters will be very honest about what they can and can't or won't do. And believe me, it's a nightmare to unpick an entire quilt full of machine-quilted stitches just because you don't like the quilting motif. Be considerate and aware of your machine quilter's time — know what you want upfront, and be clear about your wants and expectations.

Custom freehand quilting is more expensive than computerized quilting by up to six times, because it requires the quilter to move the machine themselves, using their artistic skill and steadiness to literally draw the design on your quilt with their machine and thread. Custom quilting can take dozens, even hundreds, of hours, depending on the complexity of the quilting.

If you choose to have your quilt quilted by someone else, you can still add your preferences and personality via the quilting. You may request certain thread colors, the type and style of quilting, and the batting used. If the longarm quilter you talk to isn't able to accommodate your requests, check around with other longarmers. Each is different, with varying abilities, preferences, and skill levels.

Embroidery Designs

These ten designs may be used to personalize your linens: pillowcases, sheets, or quilts. But don't stop with these! Making your own embroidery motif is as simple as making a line drawing and tracing it on to your fabric. You can even print out a word in a font you like from your computer, and trace that, for a stylized embroidery pattern. Embroidery is a beautiful way to enhance and add personality to your bed linens (Stitches on page 114). Copy and transfer to your fabric using a water solulble pen and a light source.

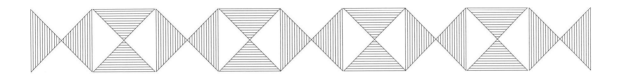

COASTAL 1

Use a satin stitch to fill in these alternating triangles. You may choose to use the same color throughout the design, or you may choose to alternate two coordinating colors. When I drew this design, I pictured it stitched in alternating navy blue and brick red on white linens, for a clean, nautical touch.

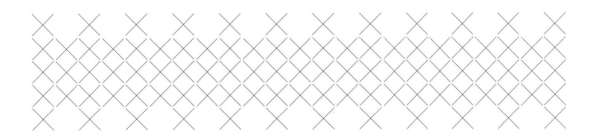

COASTAL 2

A simple, oversized cross stitch is all you need to complete this pattern. Be sure your top stitches all run the same direction for a tidy and streamlined look to your embroidery. This design could be stitched in several colors in vertical columns, or, as I imagined, using five different shades of the same color to make a fun horizontal gradient. All you need to do is start with the lightest color for the top row and work your way down, using a darker tone for each horizontal row.

FARMHOUSE 1

For a beautiful and meditative embroidery, perfect your running stitch in this design. To make a big impact, focus on making your stitches even lengths and the spaces between them consistent. I imagine this design stitched in brick red thread on taupe linen, or perhaps stitched in a navy blue on off white cotton. If you prefer using more than one thread color, I suggest using the same color in a lighter and darker tone, to maintain a cohesive feel.

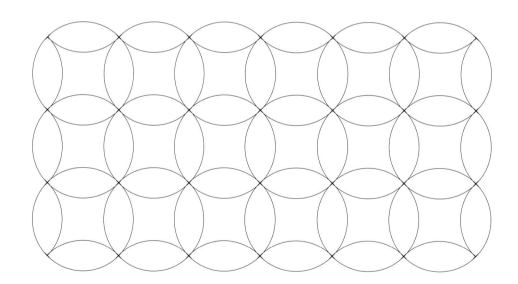

FARMHOUSE 2

Stitch the lines of this design with a small backstitch, doing your best to keep the stitch lengths consistent. If your stitches are too long, the curved lines will begin to lose their shape. This embroidery would look stunning stitched with white thread on a dark colored pillowcase or sheet, and would offer just the right "homey" touch to your bedding.

GLOBAL ECLECTIC 1

To embroider this fun paisley, you'll have to use several decorative stitches. Most of the shapes are outlined with a backstitch. Use a chain stitch on the largest paisley, french knots on the dotted border, seed stitches on the little double lines, a fly stitch for the leaf-like veining, lazy daisy stitches for the little flower, and long stitches for the stripes and crosshatching. Use a different color embroidery floss for each element for an eclectic look.

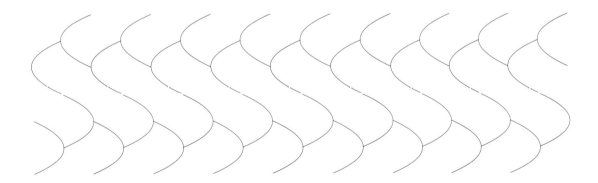

GLOBAL ECLECTIC 2

This design is worked in two rows of feather stitches, going in opposite directions. The stitch is worked from "top" to "bottom", meaning that each stitch you are making should look like a "U" with the open part up the curve toward the top of your fabric. When you complete that row, simply turn your fabric 180 degrees and work the second row in the other direction. This design would work well in gold thread on a richly saturated fabric.

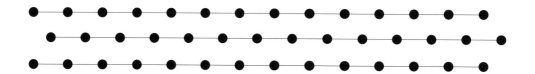

MINIMAL ZEN 1

The coral stitch runs the length of this design, in offset rows. For accuracy, it will help to mark where each knot will be placed with a water soluble marker. For added interest, you may choose to place several French knots at each "dot" for a small cluster. This design would be sophisticated in a neutral color on any background, or could be made more playful by making each row a different color.

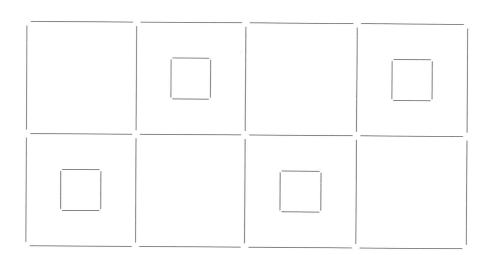

MINIMAL ZEN 2

For this simple squares embroidery, use a backstitch for the large squares, being sure to leave a small space at each intersection. For the smaller squares, use a single long stitch for each side. Alternately, you may choose to backstitch the large squares, and satin stitch the small squares for an entirely different look. Of course, you can use the same thread for the entire design, or use a different thread for the large squares and small squares.

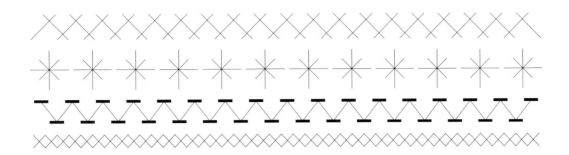

VINTAGE RETRO 1

This design reminds me of the little printed samplers I stitched as a child. Each row is a different stitch, which makes it easy to add in other lines if you'd like. The top row is made with a herringbone stitch, the second row with star stitches, the third row is the chevron stitch, and the final row is a simple cross stitch. For more detail, the herringbone, chevron, and cross stitch rows can be stitched over a cord, braid, or ribbon to hold it down.

VINTAGE RETRO 2

I inherited a similar embroidery from my husband's grandmother. It was stitched in beautiful pastels. I used a backstitch for the stems of flowers and spines of leaves. Lazy daisy stitches make up the flower petals and leaves, while the flower centers are satin stitched. Use a French knot at each large dot, and clusters of knots where there are many little dots. Finally, use a single long stitch to make the petals of the small flowers and the fern leaves.

GUIDE: EMBROIDERY STITCHES

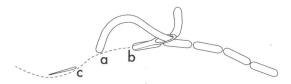

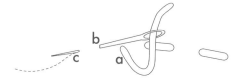

BACKSTITCH Bring needle up at (a), down at (b) where the previous stitch ended then come back up at (c) to make a continuous line. When stitching curved lines, make shorter stitches.

RUNNING STITCH Bring your needle up at (a), down at (b), and back up at (c). Keep stitches and spaces the same length.

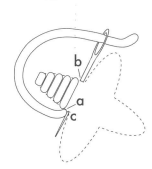

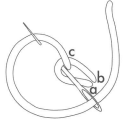

SATIN STITCH Bring your needle up at (a), down at (b), and back up again at (c). Continue in this way to fill in the shape. Be sure to keep each stitch close to the previous stitch and keep thread from twisting for a smooth look. For more dimension, backstitch just inside the outline of the shape before starting.

CHAIN STITCH Bring needle up at (a) and back down in the same hole (b) to form a loop. Needle up at (c), pulling until the loop is the shape you would like. Repeat.

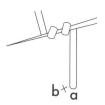 

FRENCH KNOT Bring needle up at (a), wrap thread at least twice around the needle--more times to form a larger knot. Hold thread taut and go down at (b), as close to (a) as you can. Keep the coil of wrapped thread at the surface of the fabric and pull the needle and thread through. Milliners needles work best for french knots.

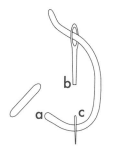 

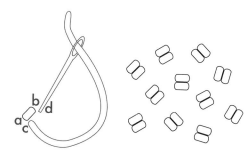

CROSS STITCH Bring your needle up at (a), down at (b), and up again directly below (c). Continue from left to right to complete the line. Then, reverse direction, working from right to left to complete the crosses.

SEED STITCH Bring needle up at (a), down at (b), up at (c) and down at (d) to make 2 parallel stitches. Continue making pairs of parallel stitches in random directions to fill in the area.

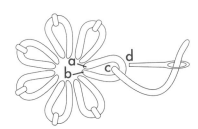

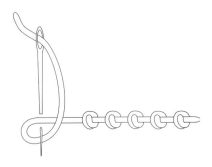

LAZY DAISY STITCH Bring needle up at (a) and back down at (b) as close to (a) as possible, leaving a loop. Needle up at (c), inside the loop. Pull thread until desired loop shape is achieved. Go back down at (d) to anchor shape. Repeat to create complete flower or leaves.

CORAL STITCH Working from right to left, bring needle up at (a). Hold thread to the left of (a). Needle down at (b) and back up again at (c). Wrap the thread around the needle from left to right. Pull the needle through the loop.

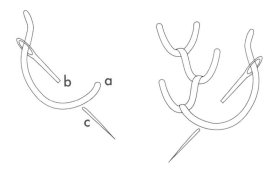

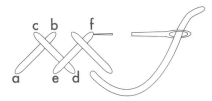

FEATHER STITCH Bring needle up at (a) and back down at (b), making a loop. Bring the needle up at (c) and pull thread to shape the loop as desired. Needle down at (d), directly to the right of (c), leaving a loop. Bring needle up at (e) and pull thread to shape loop. Repeat.

HERRINGBONE STITCH Bring needle up at (a), back down at (b), and up again at (c). Continue as needed.

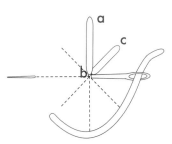

STAR STITCH Bring needle up at (a) and down at (b). Up again at (c) and back down at (b). Continue around the points of the star, always returning to point (b) after each needle up.

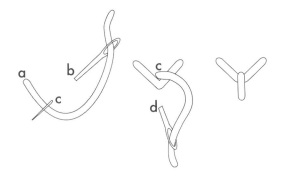

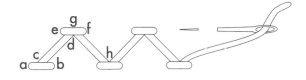

FLY STITCH Bring needle up at (a) and down at (b) leaving a loop. Come up at (c) and with the needle over the loop, pull the thread through to form a V shape. Go down at (d) to anchor the shape. Repeat.

CHEVRON STITCH Bring needle up at (a) and back down at (b). Needle up at (c), exactly halfway between (a) and (b). Needle down at (d). Up at (e), down again at (f), and up again at (g), as close to (d) as possible. Repeat.

THE LINENS

No bed is complete without coordinating sheets and pillowcases. In many respects the pillowcases and sheets are the most important part: they are the fabrics that actually touch our skin! Consider the discussions we've had on fabrics and batting, and be aware that there are many, many options for commercially purchased linens. You don't have to use just cotton! There are a variety of thread counts to choose from and organic, knit, satin, flannel, and other fibers to consider. Choose the sheets that best suit your climate, preference, and budget. We can gussy them up, too, if you'd like.

There's another option: you may choose to make your own linens — and in doing so, you open up even more options than you may have in the store.

HOW TO MAKE YOUR OWN FLAT SHEET FROM 108" WIDE YARDAGE

1 Measure the length, width, and depth of your mattress. **(Fig. 1)**

2 To determine the proper length for your flat sheet, add the following:

Length of Mattress + Depth of Mattress + 9" (top cuff) + 12" (tuck in at foot of bed)

3 To determine the proper width for your flat sheet, add the following:

Width of Mattress + Depth of Mattress + 8" (side tuck in) + 2" (side hems)

4 Trim your yardage to the measurement determined above.

5 Turn the top edge under ½" **(Fig. 2)** and press well. Turn the top edge under again 4½" and press. Stitch ⅛" away from the folded edge. **(Fig. 3)**

6 Turn the bottom edge under ½" and press. Turn the bottom edge under ½" again and press. Stitch along folded edge, as close as possible to the fold. **(Fig. 4)**

7 Repeat with left and right sides, turning each edge under ½" twice, and stitching along the folded edge.

Voila!

Making flat sheets

108"-wide yardage can be used to make flat sheets for your bed. Why bother?

First, you may have a mattress that is a different size than commercially available linens. Making your own sheets eliminates the hassle of trying to find something to fit, as you can easily adapt the measurements.

Second, if you get 108"-wide yardage on sale or clearance, it can be significantly cheaper than buying a queen- or king-size sheet set.

Third, if you can make it for your bed, you can make it for someone else's, too. Can you imagine how

adorable a custom sheet on a toddler bed would be?

While it is possible to make a fitted sheet from yardage, I don't recommend it. Fitted sheets for large beds require more than 108" of width, and having a seam through the middle of a fitted sheet could be itchy, uncomfortable, unattractive, or all three. If you have a mattress that requires more width than 108" and are determined to make your own sheets, piece the yardage needed on each side so that the seams are near the edges, or secure a middle seam by using a reinforced stitch.

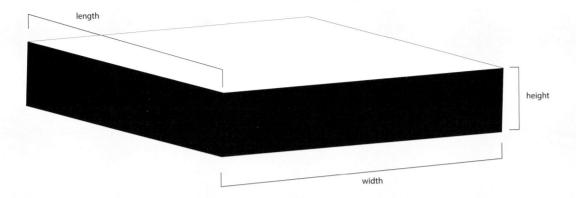

Figure 1

length

height

width

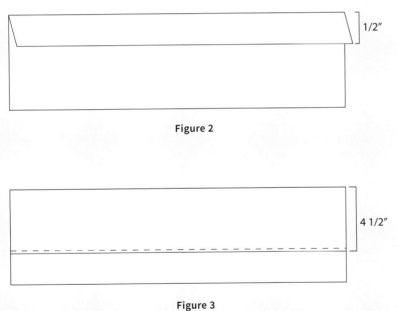

1/2"

Figure 2

4 1/2"

Figure 3

1/2"

Figure 4

NOTE: Purchase a little more (10" or so) 108"-wide yardage than you need to be long enough, according to the length measurement determined above. Remember, 108" backing is still sold by the yard, so you will likely need three or more yards. Pre-wash your fabric so that your measurements are accurate, and your sheet still fits after you wash it the first time. I suggest pre-washing your fabric the same way you plan to wash your sheets.

BASIC PILLOWCASE (STANDARD SIZE)

You can make a pillowcase out of any washable fabric that you would like to lay your head on! I use cotton pillowcases in the fall and winter and voile pillowcases in the summer (I love that they feel cold when I lay down on them).

For a standard size pillowcase you'll need 1⅛ yards of fabric. When sewing pillowcases, use a ½" seam allowance.

1 Cut a 36 ½" x 40" rectangle from your fabric. **(Fig. 1)**

2 Fold one 40" side under ½", press in place. **(Fig. 2)**

3 Fold the same side under another 4½", press in place. Stitch⅛" away from the folded edge to make a cuff. **(Fig. 3)**

4 Fold pillowcase in half, right sides together, matching up corners and cuff. Pin around the unfinished edge to keep everything in place.

5 Stitch around the pinned edge using a ½" seam allowance, pivoting at the corner. Clip the corner seam to eliminate bulk. Finish the raw-edged seam and bind loose threads by either sewing a zigzag or overlock stitch, or by using a serger around the same edge you just stitched. This will keep the seam nice through many washings. **(Fig. 4)**

6 Turn the pillowcase right side out. You're done!

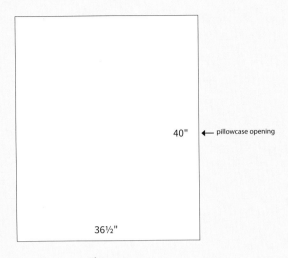

40" ← pillowcase opening

36½"

Figure 1

NOTE: Be aware that the 40" side of the rectangle is where the pillow will eventually be inserted. If you're using stripes or some other directional fabric, pay attention to how you place and cut your fabric so that it is oriented the way you would like it to be.

4 1/2"

Figure 2

1/2"

Figure 3

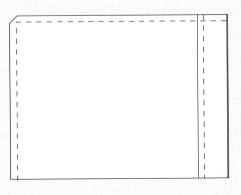

Figure 4

Embellishing linens

If you don't have the time or the inclination to make your own sheets or pillowcases, you can add personality to purchased linens as well as handmade ones.

EMBROIDERY

Just as with a quilt top, embroidery can be used to add a final touch to a pillowcase or sheet. You may choose a small motif placed somewhere prominent, like the middle of the cuff, or you may want to repeat the design to continue along the entire band of the cuff or along the top of the sheet. Be sure to secure your stitches well so that they will hold up through multiple washes.

MACHINE STITCHES

Another fun way to embellish sheets and pillowcases is with the decorative stitches on your sewing machine. Most modern machines have several, if not hundreds, of "fancy" stitches — but even if the only stitches you have are a straight stitch and a zigzag, you could run several lines of a decorative stitch along the cuff of a sheet or pillowcase. It's a fast, easy, and fun way to spice up something plain.

FABRIC

If you have a favorite fabric you would like to incorporate into your plain sheets, there's a quick and simple way!

1 Cut several widths of fabric strips at least 1½" or even a pieced block (**see photo left**) and stitch them end to end. Press seams open. Press long edges under ¼".

2 Pin the strip in place on the sheet along the bottom of the cuff (or wherever you want it), leaving 1" overage on both edges. Fold the extra 1" under ½" once, and then ½" again, so that the edge of the strip is wrapped around the edge of the sheet.

3 Stitch along both folded edges of the strip, catching the wrapped edge pieces in the seam.

You could opt to leave the edges raw, for a fun, casual raw-edge-appliqué look that will fray when washed. You could also use more strips and gather them into pleats, make little quilt blocks, or even just small squares pieced in a long strip, and stitch them to the top of your sheet using the same technique. The possibilities are endless.

Incorporating your favorite fabric in a store-bought pillowcase (see page 124) is a great way to embellish too!

TRIMS

A quick and easy custom detail to add to sheets or pillowcases is using a trim of your choice (**see photo below**). Be sure to choose something that will wash well and that isn't uncomfortable to have near your skin when sleeping.

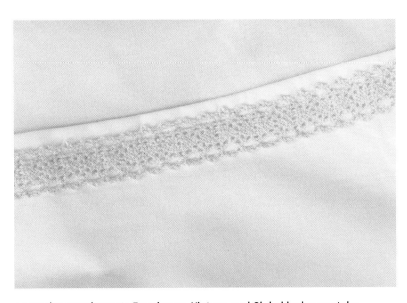

Lace trim complements Farmhouse, Vintage, and Global bedroom styles.

Custom pillowcases

Four fast and easy ways to personalize your pillowcases:

MONOGRAM

Use fusible webbing to appliqué a reverse monogram on a pillowcase. Be sure to place the monogram toward the edge of the pillow so it isn't uncomfortable to lay on. **(see photo above)**

PIECED INSERT

Create a beautiful pieced insert from your quilt scraps **(Fig. 1)**

1 Measure your pillowcase from top to bottom. Multiply that measurement by 2 and add ½".

2 Make a strip of squares or small quilt blocks that same length. Stitch the ends together to make a loop. **(Fig. 2)**

3 Lay your pillowcase out flat. With a rotary cutter, cut ½' away from the seam line inside the cuff.

4 Cut the width of your strip minus ½" from your pillowcase. For example, if the width of my pieced loop was 2½", I would cut a 2" piece out of my pillowcase. **(Fig. 3)**

5 Place the pieced loop around the cut edge of the pillowcase, right sides together. Pin.

6 Stitch with a ¼" seam allowance. Finish the seam with a zigzag or overlock stitch. Press the seam toward the pillowcase. Topstitch ¹/₁₆" from the seam to finish. **(Fig. 4)**

7 Replace the cuff by placing it right sides together with the pieced insert, lining up the cuff's side seams with the side seams of the original pillowcase. Pin and stitch in place using a ¼" seam allowance. Finish the seam with a zigzag or overlock stitch. Press toward cuff. Topstitch ¹/₁₆" from the seam.

Figure 1

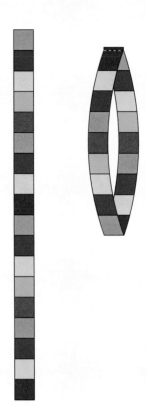

Figure 2

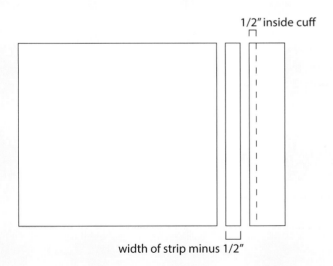

1/2" inside cuff

width of strip minus 1/2"

Figure 3

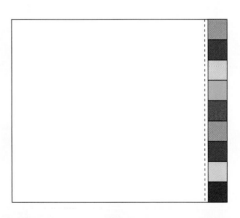

Figure 4

ADD OR REPLACE THE CUFF ON YOUR PILLOWCASE

1 Measure your pillowcase from top to bottom. Multiply that measurement by 2 and add ½".

2 Cut a strip of fabric that is 10" x (your measurement). Fold each long edge under ½" and press. **(Fig. 1)**

3 Fold the strip in half, right sides together, and stitch the two short ends together using a ¼" seam allowance. **(Fig. 2)**

4 Press seam open. Fold the loop of fabric in half, matching the long raw edges that have been turned under. Press, making sure that the raw edges are hidden between the two outside layers of fabric. **(Fig. 3)**

5 Using your rotary cutter and a ruler, cut the cuff off of your ironed pillowcase. Insert the cut pillowcase edge between the two folded edges of your new cuff about ½", making sure that the seam on the cuff is aligned with the seam on the pillowcase.

6 Stitch $1/16$" from the edge of the cuff, 1 and again ¼" from the edge of the cuff.

TRIMS

Use trim, such as ribbon, rickrack, or lace, on your pillowcase like this:

1 Measure your pillowcase from top to bottom. Multiply that measurement by 2 and add ½".

2 Cut a piece of your chosen trim to that length. Place right sides together and stitch short ends using ¼" seam allowance, backstitching several times to secure. If possible, press seam open.

3 Pin and stitch trim to desired location around pillowcase, avoiding the area that is slept on. **(Fig. 4)**

Figure 1

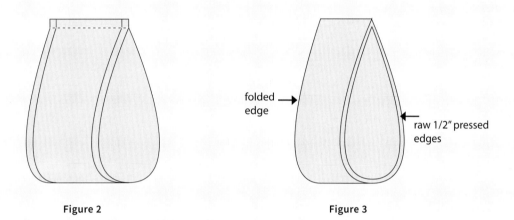

folded
edge →

← raw 1/2" pressed
edges

Figure 2

Figure 3

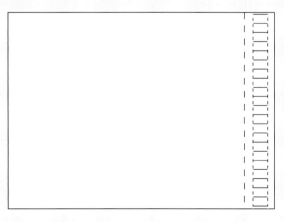

Figure 4

ACKNOWLEDGMENTS

Mom: Always my cheerleader and, even better, my friend. Thank you for teaching me that hard work pays off, that they're only little for a short while, and that kindness is always a trump card. I'm glad you won the coin toss. xoxo

Gaylene: Truly my quilting fairy godmother. Thank you for your unwavering support and love.

Lucky Spool: To Susanne, for having the faith to take on a wild card, and for your grit, guts, and vision. I am so excited to be a part of what you're creating. To Kirstin, Liz, and the other amazing ladies who help me look better and sound smarter — everyone needs an amazing team like you.

My Crafty Ladies: To Lyndi, Jillian, Kathy, Amy, Jordan, Kristen, Brooke, Sue, Sue, Robin, Stephanie, and Emily — thank you for forcing me to be social every week, and for your love and enthusiasm. Oh, and the laughs, too. I love you guys.

Moda: For being the first company that truly inspired me to create, and for believing that one person was worth encouraging. Thank you! I adore that I can call myself a part of your family.

Fabric manufacturers: For creating the beautiful fabrics that allow me to fully express my ideas in quilt form: Moda, Robert Kaufman, Andover, Studio e, Free Spirit, Dear Stella, Art Gallery, and Michael Miller.

Batting: To Erin and Darlene at Pellon — for their helpful information on batting weights and warmness — and for providing batting for all the quilts in this book.